MW00714750

ATLANTIC COASTAL GARDENING

GROWING INSPIRED, RESILIENT PLANTS BY THE SEA

Denise Adams

Nimbus Publishing Limited
3731 Mackintosh St, Halifax, NS B3K 5A5
(902) 455-4286 nimbus.ca

Printed and bound in China

NB1093

Design: Jenn Embree
All photos by Denise Adams with the exception of p. vi, provided courtesy of Dr. Robert LaRoche

Library and Archives Canada Cataloguing in Publication

Adams, Denise, 1961-, author
Atlantic coastal gardening : growing inspired, resilient plants by the sea / Denise Adams.

Includes index.
Issued in print and electronic formats.
ISBN 978-1-77108-144-3 (bound).—ISBN 978-1-77108-145-0 (pdf)

1. Seaside gardening—Atlantic Coast (Canada). 2. Coastal plants—Atlantic Coast (Canada). I. Title.

SB460.A33 2014 635.09715 C2013-907559-3
C2013-907560-7

Canada Council for the Arts Conseil des arts du Canada

Nimbus Publishing acknowledges the financial support for its publishing activities from the Government of Canada through the Canada Book Fund (CBF) and the Canada Council for the Arts, and from the Province of Nova Scotia through the Department of Communities, Culture and Heritage.

In memory of my late French Acadian father, Martial Landry

He drew from land and sea with great reverence. At sea, it was one hook for one man. In the garden, a seaweed-based compost fertilized the crops we so enjoyed. I remain forever grateful to him for showing me in my youth one of the most spectacular acts of creation on Earth...how a simple seed could grow into such heavenly flowers, even so close to the sea.

Contents

ACKNOWLEDGEMENTS

Although I have been a bit of a seaside recluse these days, I very much appreciate that a project of this magnitude always involves others. I have so many to thank. My gratitude goes first to fellow gardener—and not so long ago, neighbour—Maria Kuttner. I thank Maria for volunteering to proofread the manuscript in its early stages and for doing so in a most professional manner. From there, I had enough to present a first draft to Patrick Murphy, managing editor of Nimbus Publishing.

I am very grateful to Patrick for expressing an interest in my idea even before it was finished. This gave me the impetus to delve deeper into the practical side of coastal gardening. Many thanks go also to the talented team at Nimbus who put this book together and especially to my long-suffering editor Whitney Moran for her insights, spirit of collaboration, and for her mastery of the English language.

I am thankful to my friend, colleague, and ocean enthusiast, Isla McEachern, for reminding me over and over that one does not have to have grown up by the sea to be as passionate about it as I. To her husband, David McCarthy, I am appreciative for the great advice and assistance with photography issues. Many thanks also go to John Liddard for getting me out of digital jams and for his "sky photo" contributions from his "flying-camera invention."

My heartfelt thanks go to all the gardeners who have welcomed me into their special seaside spaces, for sharing their gardening practices, and for allowing me to take pictures whenever I felt the lighting was best. Thank you to Dr. Roger Morin and his gardening wife Susan, Olga and Vern Fredericks, Shirley Parks, Karen and Mike Yabsley, Kip and Marina Harris, Rafi Litcht and Gabrielle Applebaulm, Walter Ostrum, Leroy Hill, Peter and Marilyn Corkum, Bonnie and Bill Gimby, Peter Dodge and Cherie Neima.

To those who may find a photo of their seaside garden that I have taken from a brief drop-in, a drive-by, or from the boat, thank you so much for the amazing display and anonymous contribution. Thanks also go to our long-time family friend Melba Shute, for getting me acquainted with harvesting dulse on the shores of Fundy Bay, Nova Scotia.

Finally, I am most grateful to my husband Rick for believing in my ability to pull this project off and for enduring my extended periods of hibernation while writing. For the many times I told him that he and the dog were my greatest distraction...I take that back. In fact, Rick, you were a comfort and an invaluable support. Your sense of humour has trickled into my writing. Thank you lots.

Wharf Hags
LOCAL ARTISANS

Introduction

Why Garden at the Coast?

The Earth with its store of wonders untold...
and round it hath cast like a mantel the sea.
—Sir R. Grant—

We are so fortunate to live on land surrounded by ocean. One is never very far away from the sea in the Maritimes. Native plant life at the coast is dense, varied, and visually stunning. Coastal gardeners are inspired by such resilience. We have a profound affinity for places where land meets sea. Homeowners who are passionate about the sea are often equally passionate about gardens. For the most part, those of us who grew up by the sea are happiest in the water, on the water, or looking at the water. And then there are those folks from inland areas, often from afar, who come to the coast later in life They have decided that this peaceful land, hugged by ocean, is where they want to be. They readily and wholeheartedly embrace the maritime lifestyle. The coast is a place where we can all grow, plant, play—a place we can call our own.

Coastal gardening is not a new idea. It has been going on for a long time here by the Atlantic Ocean. Although a time-tested tradition dating back to the arrival of early settlers, it is surprising that little information can be found on the subject. A few books have been written on the topic of seaside gardens.

Little relics of life at sea animate a coastal property

So far as we can tell, they are of gardens south of the border to us, in warmer, tranquil bays. Their pages display grandiose seaside estates, designed by professionals and maintained by hired gardening staff. *Atlantic Coastal Gardening*, to the contrary, is for the hands-on gardener. It is specifically about how to grow vibrant gardens where the sea is not far from one's doorstep, where exposure to the elements is an ongoing part of life.

The Maritime coastline is peppered with such properties, especially in communities and villages with a long history of fishing and seafaring. Nova

Old fish stores are enjoyed as coastal cottages

Once the fog lifts, our attention goes to the colours of the garden.

Scotia, in particular, has experienced a trend of seaside revitalization for some time now. Family cottages are being restored, old ships' captains' houses renovated and long-standing homesteads restored. Even retired fish stores are getting a kind of refit for recreational use. Owners of these cherished dwellings, and of newer seaside homes, aspire to adorn their places with lovely, hardy gardens, and for good reason: this is an expression of what they are passionate about. Gardening engages all the senses. It provides a creative outlet. It is a means of augmenting the beauty and value of the seaside setting. Furthermore, gardening is a heart-healthy pastime. One feels rejuvenated after time spent in salty fresh air. I believe the fountain of youth may actually be found at the coast, and of course, in tending a little garden.

The coastal garden has a particular atmosphere. It renders the gardener all the more conscious of the tides, cycles of the moon, and changing seasons. The rising and setting of the sun affects the ambiance of the garden throughout the day. Early risers are eager to get out, coffee or tea in hand, to feel the morning mist and take in the visual experience of softened edges. The sea is usually still at this time of day. There is a pleasant, mysterious scent of freshly sliced cucumber in the air.

Looking to where land meets shore, grasses, flowering plants, and vines present themselves in a pastel palette. It is a joy to get out there and attend to the plants that bring so much to the experience of coastal living. Come midday, when fog lifts, the garden is under the spotlight. The high noon sun reveals brilliant colours, myriad crisp shapes, and interesting textures. At this time of the day, the garden is the stage and the sea its backdrop. When you turn your eyes toward the ocean, you notice the effects of afternoon breezes. Mesmerizing sparks of sunlight hop over swirling cobalt waters. Distant undulating swells leave trails of white seafoam. The rhythm of waves lapping the shore becomes the soundtrack for the set.

A time of reflection

Later on, all becomes still again. The water becomes a mirror to the colourful whims of the fading sky. This is a time of reflection in both senses of the word. At dusk, long, soft shadows with intermittent golden light enter our living spaces. We assess the day that we had and prepare for rest. Gardening at the coast is always time well spent.

My first seaside garden was in Boutiliers Point on St. Margarets Bay, Nova Scotia. It was a tiny lot with a few mature spruce trees and what many would call a weedy, windswept lawn. Close inspection of what was growing along the shore led to the surprising discovery of all kinds of native and naturalized flowering plants, shrubs, and vines. I immediately began to clear away the grasses from around them. This was a great base from which to visualize what else, requiring minimal care, would be able to grow there. Ocean stones, landed driftwood, retired lobster traps, and buoys became focal points. I only needed to refresh the surrounding soil and add a few hardy perennials and annual seeds to fill in the blanks.

One fine summer day, while tending my flower patches, an elderly woman known as the "community inspector" walked by. She complimented me on the lovely flowers growing along the road where she walked almost daily. I was pleased with her comments and

Campion and dropmore flowers thrive in wind and salt spray

agreed that everything was blooming gloriously. "But," I added, "it doesn't feed the world." "That may be so," she replied, "but it feeds the soul." Ms. Molten, since passed away, went on to say that she was always told that nothing could grow so close to the sea. "Watching your garden grow here at water's edge gives me a reason to get out of the house," she told me on several occasions. It was the greatest compliment I could have ever received.

Frankly, my first few coastal gardens were trial-and-error experiments. I am now on my fourth. I have had to rely to a great extent on childhood memories of summers spent with my French Acadian grandmother in her garden on the North Shore of New Brunswick. I am not the first to say this, but my grandmother's garden is the first garden I remember. She always had an abundance of colourful flowers waving in the sea breeze. The vegetable garden was a productive, engaging, and rewarding labour of love.

My father, her son, was an excellent gardener, too. He didn't talk much, but I am sure that his good gardening practices influenced the way I garden today. He was a committed composter of seaweed. His flower and vegetable gardens were luscious and impeccably kept.

Looking to what local coastal gardeners were growing was also very helpful in getting me started. I have been keeping journals and sketches of my seaside gardening experiences for a span of nearly three decades. These were all valuable resources to draw upon for writing this book.

Native blue flag irises bloom happily by the sea

This may seem to some an odd thing to say, but I have learned a lot of what I know about seaside gardening from the ocean itself. In walking various shorelines of Nova Scotia, I've noticed that native coastal plants have common characteristics. Life by the sea has caused plants to evolve to survive the elements. I believe that coastal vegetation has much to tell us about which garden plants are better equipped to grow in a seaside setting. So with this insight, I have devoted an entire chapter to my teacher, the sea, called "Lessons from Nature at the Coast." And then there are the hard-learned lessons.... As with all things in life, I learn most from my mistakes. Fortunately, my gardening successes outweigh the failures.

Gardening in proximity to the ocean does have particular challenges. But to have a coastal garden in the Maritimes is not at all impossible, nor is it a matter of settling for less. It is rather a matter of adjusting your vision of what constitutes a garden. You may think that if only a "traditional English garden" were possible here, the picture of paradise would be complete. If you are a traditionalist or tend to adorn formal gardens, be prepared to do things a little differently. Coastal gardening requires surprisingly simple methods of cultivation to achieve a bounty of healthy, hardy plants. From flowers to shrubs to vegetables, it is not complicated, but perhaps, to some, a bit unorthodox.

This is by no means a textbook. Here, readers will find not so much the basics of gardening, but rather a personable account of my coastal gardening experiences and gardening practices that I deem specific to growing plants by the sea. The core of this book is somewhat autobiographical and philosophical in nature (with a few jabs of Maritime folk humour thrown in).

Life is different out here at the coast. Seaside gardeners soon learn that we do not always have the control we would like. The Atlantic Ocean commands reverence and respect. We must learn to work with nature rather than try to alter her. The gardens featured in this book are all local with a focus on the South Shore of Nova Scotia—in particular the Peggys Cove area, where the ocean is boldest. This is because it is the place I call home. Many local gardeners will tell you that if a plant can grow in this area, it can be grown anywhere. I would have to agree. This book, therefore, speaks to all gardeners along the northeastern seaboard.

Every attempt has been made to capture the sea in photos of individual plants and coastal gardens. Sometimes, this meant compromising preferred angles and lighting. I do not at all claim to be a photographer, but what *is* in my favour, given my art background, is that I have a good sense of composition. I exercised the rule of thumb to avoid taking pictures in bright sunlight...most of the time. While garden colours are more vibrant on overcast days, the water appears dull. This was an ongoing visual dilemma (technical trickeries are above me). Furthermore, I have always felt that photography cannot do justice to the multi-sensory experience of a particular place and time, especially of life at the coast. It is my hope to fill in the gaps with words: short, thoughtful essays for the theatre of the coastal gardener's mind.

The text for this book unfolds chronologically, but one can also hop directly to a chapter of particular interest. You will find here all of my coastal gardening adventures. From great aspirations and accomplishments to disappointments and everything in between. The main mission of this book is to help you achieve success with gardening on the land that flanks the salty shores of the North Atlantic Ocean. Whether your aim is to create a garden with aesthetic appeal or for food, you will hopefully find here inspiration to get growing at the coast.

1

The Lure of Sea and Gardens

The sea, once it casts its spell, holds one in its net forever.
—Jaques Yves Cousteau—

Coastal gardening is a passion that begins with the sea. Why such a powerful lure? It is said that the forests are the lungs of the Earth. If plants are as lungs, then the ocean must certainly be the heart. The pulse of the sea is undeniable. We can see it, sense it, and hear it. This is the heartbeat that drives the rise and fall of the tides. It is as essential, constant, and rhythmic as our own heartbeat. Nutrient-rich fluids come full circle from the high seas to bays, to coves and marshes. The perpetual cycle of water feeds networks of streams and rivers that replenish lakes large and small and back again to the ocean, as reliable as the blood flowing through our veins. Yes, the ocean is indeed the heartbeat of our planet.

Ask any Maritimer why they choose to live by or make a living from the sea. No matter how remote, cold, and windy, and the answer is likely to be something along the lines of, "It is in my blood." I often heard my French-speaking relatives utter the same refrain: *La mer est dans notre sang.* I come from a long line of French Acadians who have populated the shores of New Brunswick, Prince Edward Island, and Nova Scotia since the 1700s. As a child, summer months were spent on the North Shore of New Brunswick on

Sea, sand, and stone invite beachcombing

Hollyhocks grown against a structure thrive in sea breezes

La Baie des Chaleurs. Our family had a cottage at the end of oat and potato fields that followed the shore. My summers as a youth were spent beachcombing, swimming, chasing dragonflies, and assisting my grandmother in her seaside garden. I marvelled at the miracle of food growing out of dirt, rotting seaweed, and the waste of barn animals. Although the farm garden was mostly utilitarian, *Grand-mère* Landry always found time and space to grow flowers. Her favourite was the hollyhock.

These tall flowers with stiff, sturdy stems were planted to hug the porch. They attracted an array of butterflies and hummingbirds that were sure to pay a visit to the vegetable garden before moving on. My grandmother, pointing to them, would say in her broken English: "That's a good deal!" She went on to explain to me that the butterflies and hummingbirds were doing us a free service: pollination. This was in exchange for the nectar-based energy they needed to fly south to escape Maritime winters. What an amazing and essential arrangement we have with these unassuming creatures.

Black-eyed Susans are showy flowers that grow easily by the sea.

I was the one given the honourable task of making floral arrangements for the dinner table. I combined blooms from *Grand-mère's* modest repertoire of flowers grown from seed with nearby wildflowers. The eye-catching colours, shapes, and textures of plants growing against the navy blue backdrop of the ocean made a lasting impression on me.

What a crowd arrived for lunch: several hard-working uncles and other farmhands showed up. They were all exhausted and famished! The family name "Culligan" comes to mind. This was the English-speaking Protestant family in the area whose sons worked hand-in-hand with my French Acadian Catholic uncles on the farm. Together, they focused on the task at hand: raising their families and putting food on the table, while respecting each other's cultural heritage. And of this, as an Acadian, I am very proud. With the right mindset, multiculturalism can work. Last but not least entered my workhorse of a grandfather, Henri Landry, with his manure- and mud-coated boots and ferocious appetite. I remember *Grand-mère* scolding him for eating too much, too fast.

That my grandmother's vegetable garden could feed so many, day after day, was baffling to me. It was magic from the ground! I knew, even at that tender age, that growing food and flowers at the coast was a tradition I would somehow, at some point in my life, continue. Earth and water have always had a strong tug on me. I must have a little patch of ground in which to grow something, and I must be able to see a bit of the ocean to feel whole. When I am away for just a few days, I become terribly homesick as though deprived of something essential. My garden keeps me grounded. Seeing the magnitude and power of the ocean keeps me humble. It gives me perspective.

The play between sea and sky creates a sense of wonder and awe

MORE THAN CANADA'S OCEAN PLAYGROUND

This attraction to the coast is a curious thing. Those of us who are insatiably passionate about life by the ocean most likely recall amazing childhood experiences at the shore. Others have come to the Maritimes from away; they have come for the lifestyle, peaceful and natural open spaces with easy access to ocean views, beaches, and coastlines. We call Nova Scotia "Canada's Ocean Playground," which is proudly displayed on our licence plates. But there is more to our infatuation than boardwalks and fun at the beach. We have a long history with the sea.

Human civilization began along waterways. Sea salt and seafood were two of the earliest currencies. The ocean became our highway to new worlds. We owe the beginning of globalization to the ocean. But for all its importance, we know more about the surface of the moon than we know of the depths of the ocean. According to David Suzuki, only 5 percent of the ocean floor has been mapped in detail. It is perhaps the unknown that draws us to it.

There was a globe at the back of the classroom where I landed my first teaching job. Randy, a special-needs student, enjoyed spinning it as fast as it could go, watching the colours of all the countries blend into a predominantly blue blur. One day, he asked me why this planet we call Earth turned blue when spun. "So much ocean," I answered, "way more than land." He responded brilliantly by saying: "Then this planet should have been called Ocean, not Earth!"

Young Randy had a good point. The sea after all, does cover more than 70 percent of our planet's surface. Isn't it interesting that our bodies are also about 70 percent water? We have more than a few things in common with the ocean. I wonder if the lure of the sea might have something to do with the fact that we begin life in the liquid world of our mother's womb. An expecting mother says, "My water broke" when her child is ready to enter the world. The first time a human cries is at birth. Could it be an expression of sorrow for having to leave our familiar watery world? Tears are as salty as seawater, and so far as we know, no other creature sheds them. The old proverb "blood

The mystical, life-giving sea

is thicker than water" only refers to fresh water; human blood is actually the same consistency as seawater. We are, in fact, mostly water. The human body is an ocean in itself. It runs on interdependent life systems as complex and as enigmatic as those of the ocean. I think it fair to say that we love life at the coast because the sea is so much like ourselves. Humans are as habitual as the tides, as restless as the waves, and can be as unpredictable as gale-force winds.

The sea also holds much visual interest for coastal gardeners. It is flirtatious. Bouncing flecks of light and colour entice us into the water despite the cold and onto it despite the risks. Seaside settlements charm us with their bobbing boats and slapped-together wharves with mounds of nets, traps, and pleasantly painted buoys. We cherish what remains of this traditional way of life. But with the advent of mass aquaculture and high-tech fishing, there is a sense that many of these picturesque settings will soon disappear. The greatest issue, however, is over-development. Many—at one time sustainable—large seaside lots have been subdivided over and over into parcels so small and so close together that it is nearly impossible to grow anything. Urban sprawl is fast encroaching on the serenity of our shores.

KEEPING A BALANCED RELATIONSHIP

"The Lure of Sea and Gardens" is the chapter I looked forward most to writing. This may be because I find gratification in articulating my lifelong infatuation

A serene spot to gaze at the wonders of the ocean

with the sea and with gardening. Perhaps it is because I know that I am in good company and there is satisfaction in sharing. Or, it could be because places where land meets sea have inspired so many art forms. As I gaze at the ocean, however, I am met with mixed emotions. I would be remiss not to mention the fact that the sea is finite and under unprecedented stress. How can we, in light of this troubling fact, continue to live by its side in good conscience? On one hand, I wish to sing the praises of having a seaside courtyard, and on the other, I realize that we cannot have all of humanity aspire to live by the sea. This would be an unsustainable and irresponsible promotion. Needless to say, *Atlantic Coastal Gardening* came into doubt many times during the writing process.

After several drafts, I eventually got to the heart of the matter. Simply put, living by the sea is an important part of our cultural fabric. Our relationship with the coast began as one of sustenance: settlers came to live off the land and to draw from the sea. They owe much to the sea for their survival—it was paramount in building this relatively young economy. Our economic history is not only founded upon agriculture and fishing, but also forestry, shipbuilding, military, marine, and seafaring commerce.

I believe that for the most part, our interaction with land and sea has historically been a balanced one. But with population growth comes a growth in our carbon footprint. There have been abuses in the last few decades. With awareness, however, comes restitution. We are taking steps toward conservation, perhaps too slowly, but we are making progress (more on that later). So it is in that spirit that I proceed in writing about coastal gardening. It is

The simple beauty of an untamed, untouched shore

with enthusiasm, but also with great reverence and, hopefully, discretion that I share the joys of gardening by the sea. Coastal gardening must be about living in reasonable harmony with the beautiful and powerful, yet fragile, Atlantic Ocean. To have it so near is a great privilege. It is not to be taken for granted. Now and then, when storms hit, we are once again reminded of who is in command—that we humans are, to the ocean, as insignificant as blades of grass on the shore.

NOVA SCOTIA WATERCOURSE BUFFER REQUIREMENTS

We humans have become very good at taming, shaping, and altering the bounty of this planet to our advantage. Not counting insects and microbes, humans now account for one of the highest populations on Earth, and it is growing exponentially. With population growth comes development of our planet. Nova Scotia is no exception. The days of infilling marshes, moving streams, putting in seawalls, and ripping out native vegetation from the water's edge in favour of new construction have come to an end.

The most pressing concern involves the many homes whose untreated septic still ends up at sea. As of late, proper systems must be installed as these properties change hands. New bylaws intended to protect coastlines from overdevelopment continue to be drafted. Nova Scotia (the only province I can speak of) is in the process of improving protective measures

The health of the sea is essential to the overall health of the planet.

to ensure a reasonable future balance between human activity and coastal habitats. No reshaping, infilling, or relocation of waterways is permitted.

In 2005 a new construction bylaw was drafted, which states that developers must now leave a 20-m (66 ft.) watercourse buffer to water's edge, where no excavating whatsoever is permitted. All manner of native plants, stones, and trees in this "watercourse buffer" must, by law, be left untouched, with only limited human activity. Examples of acceptable alterations within the buffer of newly constructed waterfront homes are: a narrow boardwalk to the shore, a hammock, a small deck, or a 4.5-m (15 ft.-) slipway—for which a permit is required. Permits for putting in new wharves are now very difficult to obtain. There is a long list of requirements to comply with, and if you don't, you will be issued papers and be forced to tear down. Long gone are the days of do-as-you-please on your own waterfront. For a summary of *Nova Scotia Watercourse Setback Restrictions and Stewardship*, visit gov.ns.ca/coast/ or contact a local land survey firm.

Nova Scotia has finally approved very stringent regulations for development over or near wetlands. Today, you cannot so much as remove a bulrush from its natural habitat. Variances only apply to extremely

Beach grass at sundown

unique situations. Should a portion of a marshland be decimated in favour of a development project for example, a wetland of equal size must be recreated elsewhere in Nova Scotia at the landowner's expense, under the supervision of Ducks Unlimited Canada. It is very important to be well informed before breaking ground for any kind of development. (Additional information is available at novascotia.ca/nse/wetland/docs/Development_and_Wetlands.pdf.)

The sea calls us to exercise good stewardship of our coastal lands. Fortunately, gardening with native plants is gaining acceptance and becoming a growing interest. Like it or not, native coastal plants are an inevitable part of the contemporary seaside garden palette for new coastal homes. This is not to suggest homeowners leave their oceanfront properties completely to nature's whims, gardening always involves introducing some non-native plants and artistry. Ornamental plants provide amazing visual interest and can do so with minimal interference to the natural balance of life at the coast.

The challenge of coastal gardening is being aware of what will survive the extremes of seaside weather conditions. In the next chapter, "Lessons from Nature at the Coast," I discuss the unique charm of native coastal plants and what a gift they are to the seaside gardener.

When I sit for a while in my seaside garden, I am often reminded of this quote by novelist Iris Murdoch: "People from a planet without flowers would think we must be mad with joy the whole time to have such things about us." Surely the same can be said of people from a planet without oceans. So when gardening at the coast, be mindful of the ocean's mighty role in the overall health of the planet. It is the heartbeat that holds everything together. Life on this planet could not exist without its oceans.

2

Lessons from Nature at the Coast

The very soul of a garden is shriveled by zealous regimentation…
a mania for neatness, a lust for conformity—and away go atmosphere and sensuality.
—Mirabel Osler—

I used to have a view of a sturdy stand of stunted mature apple trees at water's edge across the cove from where I live. They were multi-trunked with tightly tangled, craggy branches, a fine example of naturalization. These quaint, shrubby trees produced loads of tasty little red-green apples by late fall. Once the deer had their fill, I would collect some for my high school art students to draw from observation in a light source. The little apples made a great subject and students enjoyed the follow-up snack.

One morning, I awoke to the alarming sound of a chainsaw. The new owner of that property had decided to do away with the little old orchard. I felt an unspeakable sense of loss. In human years, it had taken at least two generations of wrestling with the ocean climate for the saplings to grow into such prolific, fruit-bearing trees. They did not obstruct the view of water from the owner's house atop the hill. These trees were clearly unappreciated—I suspect because they did not conform to the "perfect" symmetrical shape we find in garden centres today. They most likely fell into the category of plants perceived as "weed"—any and every plant

A productive apple tree at water's edge

that has not been bought or intentionally planted—a scourge to be eradicated.

CHALLENGING THE DEFINITION OF "WEED"

I must state from the start that I am a great proponent of keeping certain plants that have established themselves here naturally; especially trees, if you are so fortunate to have them. The ever so common black spruce has a distinctive appearance at the coast, certainly not a groomed one, but a look that was worthy of being painted by several members of the Group of Seven. Sometimes it takes famous artworks to get people to appreciate a certain aesthetic. Native vegetation gives the coastal garden distinction; these plants, especially tall grasses, set these gardens apart from the rest. It is refreshing to have something other than the typical wall-to-wall carpet of mowed lawn. Meandering paths through natural vegetation are so much more interesting (and maintenance-free) than flat, open, monocultural spaces.

Coastal grasses are just as wonderful as ornamental grasses.

A sumptuous wild blackberry bush

A young fox prepares to lunge at a shorebird

I would like to challenge a particular notion of "weed." All references to what my students called "weed" aside, a certain class of plants are undesirable because they either have no visual appeal or they compete too aggressively with the plants we traditionally cherish. But many naturally occurring plants are worthy of being embraced as an asset to the coastal garden.

Before making any decisions about landscaping and gardening on your oceanfront property, take stock of what is already growing. To some people, a plant whose name is unknown is either feared or unappreciated. Take time to visualize the potential that existing native and naturalized plants may have for complementing your dream of a seaside garden. The best part is that these plants take care of themselves. Native plants are, by definition, plant species whose range in the Maritimes precludes the time of European contact (1500–1600 AD). They are indigenous to specific geological areas and are specialists at growing in the conditions under which they have evolved. They have been through it all, and therefore are the most reliable plants you could hope for.

Naturalized plants are essentially garden plants that may or may not have been introduced intentionally. They could have originated from far away places centuries ago by early explorers and immigrants who came with crop seeds and animals whose hay likely contained wildflower seeds. Perhaps seeds were dropped off by stormy winds, even bird droppings, or more recently, seeds could have hitched a ride between a vehicle's tire treads. Whether annuals, biennials, or perennials, these plants establish themselves readily and return year after year if comfortable enough in their new location.

Back to the subject of indigenous plants, the native northern bayberry bush (see p. 71), for example, is a hallmark of coastal resilience: it serves as a windscreen that protects less hardy plants from damaging winds and salt spray. Thorny plants also grow in abundance along the shore. Brambles are the warriors of the coast. They battle the advancing enemy, erosion, brought on by fierce storm-surge waves. The mean reputation of these prickly plants is unfounded. They happen to be an important refuge for shorebirds to roost and nest, where they are safe from predators like owls, foxes, and cats. Who among us has not stopped to smell a wild rose or snack on the fresh raspberries and blackberries that grow so prolifically along the shore?

Plant life abounds in the barrens of Peggys Cove

SURVIVORS OF THE ELEMENTS

The geology and topography of Maritime coastlines vary greatly, but one thing is sure: every nook and cranny along untouched shores is dense with plant life. Even where the ocean is boldest, as on the barrens of the Peggys Cove Preservation Area, the diversity is surprising. Several of these plants are unique to the coast. Knowing all their identities is not as important as their role at the coast and the visual impact of their colours, shapes, and textures. The dramatic posture of trees and shrubs tell stories of feats of survival. Huge granite boulders and their fragments are tossed about over a mosaic of vegetation. The juxtaposition of fragile coastal plants and rugged stone set against the deep blue ocean is mystifying. This natural place is a visual experience of unparalleled beauty.

It is worth taking a close look at some of these resilient coastal-environment dwellers, and seeking out which distinguishing features have contributed to their survival in such climactic extremes. I am no botanist, just a keen observer. Whenever I visit the

A resilient coastal spruce carved by wind and salt spray

shore, I can't help but notice certain trends among the plants that live there. I wonder what lessons they might have for us seaside gardeners. Specifically, I ask what similar plants are best to grow by the sea, and how should they be planted?

Some plant characteristics appear to be reactions to the climate while others are adaptations. The squatting spruce trees so typical of the Peggys Cove barrens are a good example of a reaction to the elements, while plants that have adapted, like beach pea, with its succulent silver-mint-coloured leaves and stems are unique to the coast. Whether one or the other, I believe that observing plants in their natural habitat offers insight for when the time comes to select plants for your coastal garden.

Allow me to take you along this bold coastline. Intuition tells me that there are particular physical features that enable these plants to survive the elements. In the following section I zero in on certain "coastal characteristics" I have observed in shore-dwelling plants.

A reaction to the coastal climate

Plants with short, stiff needles

Bright green juniper branches spring upward like little fireworks; loosely hung, they allow brisk winds through with little impact. The most common trees to succeed along the coast are the conifers black spruce, jack pine, and tamarack. All three have short needles, even jack pine. They are remarkably robust despite obvious signs of stress from the elements. Some sport yellow-green needles on a dwarfed contorted form. In a group, they appear as synchronized dancers in a pose, leaning away from the water.

Seaside juniper

Plants that tolerate pruning

If you have ever driven along the Peggys Cove Preservation Area of Nova Scotia, you will have noticed the low-growing vegetation. Persistent onshore winds, salt spray, and poor, shallow soil are what cause this dwarfing. This is sometimes called wind pruning or wind carving. I like to call it the "bonsai effect" because the sea does naturally what

This dwarfed pine is at least ten years old.

is considered to be an art in the Orient: the intentional dwarfing of a tree or shrub by a special process of pruning branches. (Roots are also clipped and the plant is kept in a small, constricting pot.) These expressive little marvels, as with many plants found along the coast, can be several decades old. Inland, the same specimens of similar age are exponentially taller with a shape distinctive of the cultivar where wind pruning doesn't occur.

Deciduous trees such as maple, birch, and oak do well in acidic soil, but without sufficient soil depth and protection from fierce onshore winds, their attempts to settle are short lived. Now and then, however, there is an exception to the rule. It is surprising to discover a lone dwarfed maple tree on the barrens. Yet some have managed to set root, usually near a ditch where soil depth is improved and wind passes overhead. Such a broad-leafed specimen must have begun as a juvenile in a microclimate, where it was able to adjust slowly under the protection of another larger plant, a large rock, or a landed item, like part of a boat or a fish crate. (For more on microclimates, see chapter 12).

PLANTS WITH SMALL, THICK LEAVES

Clusters of shrubby deciduous plants such as mountain laurel and viburnum grow in abundance here,

Winterberry, or Canadian holly

Native beach roses

especially the lovely winterberry, also known as Canadian holly, with its brilliant red berries that stand out from the crowd in late fall and well into winter. An array of knee-high bushes grow happily in tight clusters. Like emperor penguins huddled together on an ice floe, they tell me that there is safety in numbers. Among these are lamb's kill, Labrador tea, and wild azalea. By far, my favourite native coastal shrub is the fragrant bayberry bush with its hard, frosty-blue fruit that clings tightly and closely to the stems.

PLANTS WITH PRICKLY OR THORNY BRANCHES

Brambles grow in abundance at the coast. Wild raspberries, blackberries, beach rose, and buckthorn may be impenetrable, but their thorny stems and branches provide small creatures with a refuge from predators. These prickly plants can grow on the steepest of banks right up to the water's edge and their dense, tangled growth forms wind barriers that shelter more delicate plants at the other end. Bramble bushes also play an important role in delaying erosion. Their flowers attract a diversity of pollinating insects and the fruit is an essential food source for wildlife.

Sea lavender in bloom

Native blue flag iris growing among beach grass

Plants with scaly leaves

Low-growing cedars, native false cypresses, wild heaths, and heathers share their spaces with another scaly plant: the lovely sea lavender. Look for sea lavender at the edge of tidal pools mid-August, when its mauve display of florets may cause your heart to skip a beat.

Plants with a short stature and/or creeping habit

Various red, blue, and maroon berries seem to hover atop low, leafy ground covers, many of which are well-known edibles: wintergreen, goose berries, wild cranberries, and, of course, native lowbush blueberries, to name a few. Staying low to the ground provides these delicate plants cover from fierce, damaging winds.

One of many berry-bearing coastal ground covers

Plants with grassy or reed-like leaves

It is always a pleasant surprise to come across blue flag irises in late June. Although shorter than usual at water's edge, they bloom profusely from tight, salty peat crevices in granite bedrock. Their broad, grassy leaves, together with bulrush and sea oats, sway like maestros' wands in the breeze. A steady supply of seabird waste and rotting kelp provides their poor growing medium with the nutrients they need to thrive.

Plants with fleshy, succulent leaves and stems

This low-growing, bright yellow-green succulent always gets my attention. Much like our garden variety of stonecrop, it has thick, moisture-filled, fleshy leaves that keep it hydrated in scorching salty winds.

Succulent plants have water-retaining abilities that guard against scorching salty winds.

Sea lungwort growing on a stony shore is a pleasant surprise.

Beach dusty miller has many coastal characteristics.

Plants with silvery leaves

Plants with minty-green or silvery foliage are a common sight at the shore. The colour is thought to deflect the intensity of light coming from all directions: the sun, the water, and bouncing off white sand and stone. These plants are often succulents, which means their leaves and stems act as little water reservoirs in the presence of dehydrating salt spray. Sea lungwort is a gem that puts out humble, sweet-smelling blue flowers that are easily missed unless you look closely.

Plants with fuzzy or hairy leaves

Here and there, in loose granite grit where nothing else would dare set root, are clusters of beach dusty miller hanging on for dear life. Soft to the touch, this plant seems out of place, as it looks so much like the garden variety of dusty miller and artemisia silver mound. This plant almost has it all: It is short enough to avert lashing winds. Fuzzy leaves trap and stop salt particles from dehydrating it. When the underlying grit shifts, causing the plant to lose a few roots and limbs, it tolerates the pruning nicely and generates new shoots in no time. Its minty-green leaves deflect the intensity of sunlight, and also swell after it rains, reserving water for when moisture is unavailable to the roots.

The way in which these coastal native plants have managed to cope and thrive here is brilliant. Together, they have the rich texture and vibrant colours of a fine hand-hooked Nova Scotia rug, a doormat to a sea of astounding beauty, too precious to walk on. Always stay on the footpaths, and don't pick!

A footpath on the barrens guides our way to the sea.

A CLEVER APPROACH TO COASTAL GARDENING: WALTER OSTRUM

Here is a seaside garden that left me speechless when I came upon it. What a privilege it was to meet coastal gardener, Walter Ostrum. A ceramics artist and former teacher at the Nova Scotia College of Art and Design University, he is a gardener with vision worth mentioning.

His stunning garden paradise grew from an impoverished, lifeless moonscape by the sea. The lot had been stripped of native vegetation to keep a few cows back in the 1970s. But Walter was not deterred by the stark appearance of this oceanfront lot. He saw gardening potential immediately. The first order of business was to improve the shallow, rocky soil. Seaweed was key in restoring soil fertility and depth (see before and after pictures pp. 96–97). With ameliorated soil conditions came fascinating native plants that thrived by the sea. Walter was astonished by the beauty and resilience of coastal plants and embarked on a journey, discovering what else could survive the seaside setting he was so passionate about. He did this by first looking to naturally established plants by the sea: spruce, larch, juniper, viburnum, mountain laurel, and native azalea to name but a few. He went so far as to learn their Latin names, and from there searched for cultivars of the same genome.

What is most impressive about Walter's plants is that they blend into the natural scenery as though they have always been there. What has been planted, how, and why, is quite interesting. Walter's approach to gardening is the very premise of this book. He looked to nature itself to find out what could

An early spring day in Walter Ostrum's garden

Plants well suited to coastal conditions

successfully be grown at the coast. He had the good sense to grow only plants that are suited to coastal conditions: relentless wind, spells of cool, damp, foggy days, extreme freeze-thaw episodes, and salt spray. Walter's well-established collection of plants needs no special attention. The magnificent trees, shrubs, ground covers, and flowering perennials take care of themselves. They need no winter protection—like burlap tents or layers of straw or spruce-bow coverings—or other such labour-intensive measures.

The ever-so-common mountain laurel, for example, is of the same family as the azalea and rhododendron. Walter sought out world-renowned horticulturist and hybridizer of rhododendrons and magnolias, the late Captain Steele, his mentor. Not so long ago there were only two or three varieties of rhododendron that could survive our Maritime climate. But because of Captain Steele's work and that of others to follow, we now enjoy a much greater

Native mountain laurel in bloom

Wild coastal azaleas

selection. This is the case for the vast array of plant varieties we find in garden centres today. Each had its "ancestral" start in a natural setting. So Walter chose plants with origins from climates that match that of our Maritime coast. Some of his specimens have origins from faraway places like China and Russia, but they have the fortitude to live and thrive here because they come from a climate similar to ours, and thus have physical characteristics that enable them to survive seaside conditions.

Seasoned gardeners like Walter can think of many garden-variety plants that fit this bill. That is the direction in which we are going. There are a few more crucial factors to consider when selecting plants for oceanfront gardens. The following chapter addresses why many garden-centre plants will not make it at the coast. The first step is to choose your plants well. The "coastal characteristics" identified earlier in this chapter serve as a guide for selecting cultivars that stand a much better chance of life by the sea.

IMPATIENS
$5.75
CLEM'S
IMPATIENS
'Accent Mystic Mix'
$5.75
CLEM'S
Elfin Coral'
$5.75
CLEM'S
MARIGOLD
'Durango Bee'
$5.75

3

Purchasing Plants for the Coastal Garden

A perennial is a plant that would have come back year after year if it had survived.
—author unknown—

The days are finally getting longer and warmer. Come spring, there is no greater thrill than seeing garden centres pop up along roadsides and in supermarket parking lots. After sitting through a winter that felt like it would go on forever, the brilliant colours of fresh greenhouse plants are incredibly invigorating and inspiring. Gardeners anticipate each new growing season to be better than the previous. We are eager to add to what was. I must confess that not so long ago, I was a garden-centre junkie. I used to be a bit impulsive when the sun was out on a fine spring day. With my windbreaker slung over one arm, handbag over the other, I salivated as I strolled the aisles, thinking, *A little more of this plant and a little more of that plant would be such an improvement to last year's garden*. But I have to admit that certain rash decisions for my seaside garden were disastrous.

Display that nurtures the impulse to buy

PURCHASES GONE WRONG: EXPLAINED

One of my favourite activities over the long winter months is to surround myself with gardening magazines and seed-and-bulb catalogues. I get my sketchbook out, doodle new garden plans, and then dream. I crave getting outside to begin creating something new and exciting. One winter, I read somewhere that blueberries were a great seaside plant for their tasty, antioxidant-rich berries. They were also promoted for their display of brilliant red fall foliage. This rang true to the new seaside gardener that I was, as I had noticed them growing naturally by the sea in our area. I had a vision of myself eating a bowl of cereal on the deck overlooking the ocean while picking fresh blueberries right off the bush.

The thought became an obsession. One warm, sunny May afternoon, I came upon six potted tall blueberry bushes loaded with blooms in a mall garden centre. They were pricey, but I felt they would be a good long-term investment. I bought four. I did everything right. I checked to see that the plants were not root-bound. I got different varieties for good cross-pollination. And, with great reluctance, I snapped off the blooms to encourage strong root establishment the first year.

After two weeks, the leaves were experiencing windburn. Three weeks in, hurricane-force winds completely defoliated them. By July, I thought there might be hope: the scrawny bushes were putting out new buds! A few days later, following a night of rough seas, the salt-sprayed green buds went from yellow to brown and down to the ground. I was devastated. My tall blueberry plants had been so healthy...what went wrong? They were supposed to be a good candidate for the coast.

In a last-ditch attempt to save them, I decided to move the dead-looking bushes to the vegetable

Young, immature plants have a better chance at surviving the coastal climate.

garden, which is protected from such direct hits by the ocean. The following spring, the branches were completely dead, but a few leaves were showing up at the base of three of the plants. It took those survivors another two years to yield a handful of berries.

They are doing well now. In short, these store-bought plants were not acclimatized to our coastal conditions, and the fact that they are relatively tall plants was problematic.

I can't think of a coastal gardener who doesn't have a similar story of a purchase gone wrong. The fact is, plants we find in many retail shops are mass produced. This is big business on an industrial scale. Trees, shrubs, and flowering plants are started in massive climate-controlled greenhouses and are grown in ideal conditions for maximum-speed growth. If they see the light of day at all, it is likely in a warmer, gentler climate than ours. These plants are then groomed to perfection—into ideal symmetrical forms—and their blooms are often "forced" (through the use of artificial manipulation of light and darkness and fertilizers that induce premature blooming) to show their best colours on time for the market. They arrive at garden centres by the pallet, stacked up high in transport trucks. Their trip could have covered a radius from as far away as Mexico, across the US to British Columbia, and over to inland Ontario before they arrive in the Maritimes. The plants are then unloaded, grouped in layers, and arranged in contrasting colours to seduce the potential consumer.

The very conditions that draw us to the sea are far from the originating conditions in which these plants are grown. Many of these pampered, nursery-grown plants are hardly ready to face Atlantic Canadian climate conditions, much less life by the sea. That money-back guarantee will not apply if your plant perishes due to environmental factors. When you return a dead plant, you are expected to prove that you were sold a sick plant. For an additional cost, some nurseries offer insurance packages on perennials, but avoiding rushed decisions is the better course to take.

PERIL PREVENTION

Ideally, you want hardy, showy plants that are able to survive shallow acidic soil, hurricane-force winds, salt spray, long spells of fog, deer invasions, sudden freeze and thaw, cold hard rains, periods of low rainfall,

A well-stocked favourite loacal nursery in St. Margarets Bay, Nova Scotia

storm surges, and to top it all off, plants that will keep going despite neglect on your part. Sounds like this could only be some kind of coastal cactus, doesn't it? Well, my mother-in-law found the perfect solution: wood tulips, plastic mums, and silk geraniums. They look great year-round, even in the snow!

Have no worries, this ole Newfie is a good sport. The point here is that in the Maritimes, right on the coast, we have to choose our plants well.

There are advantages to buying plants from smaller, local nurseries. First of all, many of their plants are propagated and grown in the province or state in which they operate. While these stores typically don't import stock on a grand level, their shelves are kept replenished with fresh arrivals throughout the season. Staff is usually very knowledgeable and happy to share their invaluable practical advice. Big box garden centres, on the other hand, are often staffed with low-paid seasonal workers who do little more than keep plants watered and run the cash register.

When it comes to plant identification, plant habit, sun/shade requirements, soil acidity needs, perennial, biennial, and annual designations, many staff in these larger garden centres fall short. The employee overseeing the operation is the person to go to with your inquiries (hopefully). It has been my experience, however, that this person is often not on site (even when I was told that he or she would be in the next day—which did not materialize).

You may have noticed that those large parking-lot garden centres are temporary, torn down mid-season as quickly as they went up. This is not necessarily because sales are slow but more likely because the plants have become sad and unruly from lack of care, and

Fall selection at Seabright Greenhouses

many have become fatally root-bound. This is when the big "bargains" hit. If you are a bargain hunter, be very choosy, and beware of such deals:

- ALL ANNUALS: $ .50
- ALL PERENNIALS: $1.00
- ALL TREES AND SHRUBS: $5.00.

PLANT PURCHASING CHECKLIST

All stages of the growing season bring me clients for landscape consultation. It is important for me to take them along to a local plant store for two reasons: to get a sense of what they like, in a well-maintained establishment stocked with healthy plants, and to take their business to nurseries owned by residents of our region, supporting the economic imperative to buy local. There are always a few novelty plants on display. My new-to-gardening clients tend to gravitate immediately toward exotics, so they appreciate my advice on wiser choices for their oceanfront properties. Keeping their seaside gardens manageable and successful is our goal (see chapter 5).

Plants grown and sold in your coastal area will certainly have a head start on living by the sea. In other words, avoiding exotics should be first on your checklist of what to look for while shopping. The following are other helpful tips in choosing plants better suited to seaside conditions.

Choose Younger, Potted Plants

When shopping, there is a temptation to go for the tallest and biggest plants available. Everyone wants that instant effect of an established garden. However, keep in mind that younger plants have not been coddled as long as the bigger, more mature specimens.

Choose small, young potted plants over large, mature specimens.

Saplings will certainly require more time to achieve that desired "established" look, but they are more flexible and easier to shelter in the event of a storm, while they struggle to get strong roots down. Younger plants do better at establishing themselves at the coast than the more mature ones. You can't teach an old *plant* a new trick either. In other words, the more mature the plant, the less able it is to adapt to drastic new conditions.

Choose Dwarf Specimens

These days, gardeners have access to myriad cultivars. The diversity can be overwhelming. Many types of commonly known trees and shrubs have been developed to stay small or grow very slowly. These are often referred to as dwarf specimens, or, as in the case of the Japanese maple, some are called tall shrubs as they are not truly trees. Because of their short stature and gradual growth, these plants stand a better chance at surviving the climactic conditions of exposed oceanfront properties. Since they are slow to grow, they take longer to propagate to a marketable size. As a result, dwarf plants tend to be expensive, but they are worth the investment. Look to a reputable local nursery and ask for dwarfed plants that have wintered outside in a climate that approximates your own.

New dwarfed varieties are being developed every year: dwarf trees, evergreen shrubs, ornamental foliage shrubs, and flowering shrubs are becoming more and more popular in miniature forms. The Latin names of these varieties often have one of the following suffixes: ***minima***, ***compressa***, ***gnom***, ***compacta***, and ***horizontalis***. Keep in mind that the ideal time to plant at the coast, if at all possible, is when dwarf varieties—or any plant for that matter—are still in winter dormancy. That is, before they have begun to open their new buds.

Fresh, new growth is tender and risks wind damage at the coast. The buds of potted plants in a nursery

Japanese maple is a very small ornamental tree that thrives by the sea.

Planted young, this globe cedar (right) will grow to 1 m (3 1/3 ft.) in width and height at the coast.

can open almost completely on just one good day. But at the coast, buds need to open slowly and cautiously over a period of several days or weeks. It is better for a tree or shrub to have the seaside climate dictate when to come alive. June and July are safe months for introducing potted plants to the seaside garden, but they will have had less time to become established before hurricane season. Protection that first year is advised if plants are in an exposed area.

Choose Plants with Coastal Characteristics

The ten coastal characteristics identified in chapter 2 (p. 23) apply to all plants: perennials, biennials, and annuals. Most gardeners strive for lots of colour in the coastal garden, so I will give some attention here to flowering plants and offer examples of which physical features to look for.

Annuals deserve special mention for the coastal garden. They are great choices because they remain in bloom all season and are taken up when Old Man Winter arrives. Annuals are an immediate solution to enhancing a dull spot or filling in gaps between young perennials, trees, and shrubs that need time

Fall-blooming sedum sport several coastal characteristics.

Impatiens and lobelia are low-growing annuals that infill the gaps between young perennials nicely.

to mature. Because annuals are not generally hardy, gardeners need not be concerned with zone hardiness when planting them. I prefer to grow my own annuals from seed (see chapter 4) because I enjoy the impact of a lot of one colour, and otherwise this would mean buying more plants than I am willing to pay for. If you don't grow your own, choose young, perky, low-growing, compact annuals from garden nurseries. Tired-looking, gangly plants will not likely survive the slightest onshore wind, nor will tall varieties.

Spectacular statice is an everlasting that grows extremely well by the sea.

dried statice

Many annuals sport one or more coastal characteristics (see p. 23). Statice, as an example, has woody stems with serrated sides—somewhat thorny, but not truly sharp. It is short and bushy, stands up well to coastal winds, and tolerates poor soil. As a bonus, this plant comes in every colour of the rainbow and is an "everlasting." Dried, it holds its colours for years. I have discovered that annuals meant for part-sun are much better suited for life by the sea. As with plants with a low hardiness zone, these annuals, too, fare well in long stretches of fog and also tend to prefer soil that is slightly more acidic—one of the effects of fog and salt spray.

When buying biennials, remember that you are dealing with flowering plants in their second year of growth. They will not return the following year, but seeds can be easily collected (from most species). The next chapter is where you will find my method for starting biennials from seed.

Many, many perennial flowers are good candidates for the coast. Again, those tolerant of partial shade and that have one or more of the coastal characteristics will thrive. Any of the succulents, such as sedums, stonecrops, and honeysuckle, are excellent choices. I have listed more tried-and-true favourites at the end of the book (see Appendix, p. 224).

Honeysuckle grows exceptionally well by the sea.

CHOOSE PLANTS AT LEAST TWO ZONES LOWER THAN YOUR AREA

Garden centres offer so many cultivars to pick from these days I feel like a novice. So many new and unfamiliar plants line the stands each year. I wouldn't be surprised to learn that some originated in faraway, tropical places. The next most crucial factor to consider when shopping for plants intended for a coastal garden is the zone-hardiness label—even though the Plant Hardiness Zone Map published by Agriculture Canada is lacking in many respects when it comes to the Maritime coast. There really should be a hardiness zone map drawn up that is specific coastal areas of the Maritimes, as they vary tremendously in climactic extremes.

Wind, salt spray, and the frequency of extremes in specific coastal regions have not been factored into the Plant Hardiness Zone Map. So when looking to buy perennials destined for an exposed oceanfront property, a good rule of thumb is to go with plants labelled at least two zones lower than what has been prescribed for your general area.

ZONING IT DOWN

Plant hardiness zones are established according to the average winter temperature in a region, the length of periods without freezing, levels of precipitation, degree of humidity, and the velocity of dominant winds. There are ten zones, each given a number from zero to nine, with zero being the coldest and nine being the warmest. Each zone is then divided into sub-zones, with sub-zone "a" slightly colder than sub-zone "b" (see plantmaps.com).

All plants obviously have a certain tolerance for extremes of cold and heat. At the coast, these extremes are both more severe and frequent. Garden centres in Nova Scotia, for example, stock plants labeled zone 6b and down because most hardiness-zone maps place Nova Scotia between zones 5a and

Ferns are cold-hardy, shade-tolerant plants: ideal for the coast.

6b, for which -20 degrees Celsius (-4 Fahrenheit) is the coldest temperature for certain areas and 0 degrees Celsius for others (notably the South Shore). However, these are mere averages. The headwaters of St. Margarets Bay may very well be zone 6b, but good luck if you buy a zone 6b plant and live in Peggys Cove, situated at the mouth of the bay, where a windy winter day is more like zone 4a of Northern New Brunswick.

Plant hardiness zone maps are generic. They are not a reliable guide for certain parts of the coast where, more often than not, there is little to no snow cover, and where the wind chill factor goes off the charts. Summers are moist and cool, and winters are relatively mild when winds are down. Lower-zoned plants tend to do better in temperature and climactic conditions with extreme fluctuations. They can cope with being fogged in for days at a time as well as with spells of intense sunlight that result in drought-like conditions. They can also better survive sudden and frequent events of freeze and thaw so typical of North American seaside winters. These plants also prefer slightly acidic soils (see chapter 8). Furthermore, plants classed within a lower hardiness zone tend to have one or more coastal characteristics (see p. 23).

If your new plants are destined for an adequately sheltered spot, you have a bit more flexibility in choice

Hydrangeas prefer acidic soils and filtered light, but require winter protection—especially at the coast.

of plants to buy. In such cases, you need only be aware of the zoning for your general area, keeping in mind sun/shade requirements. Otherwise, "Zone It Down." My area (near Peggys Cove) and the South Shore of Nova Scotia, for example, are given a general hardiness zone of 6a to 6b. So I am careful to choose plants suited to zones 4a or lower. I also avoid long-range zones. If looking for a suitable forsythia, for instance, I would bypass forsythia "Fiesta" (zones 4 to 9) and give preference to "Northern Gold" forsythia (zone 3).

Below is a summary of what to look for when buying plants for a seaside garden in an exposed coastal area. Keep this mental checklist of what to look for when shopping for garden plants.

When purchasing plants for the seaside garden, always choose:

- Younger, potted plants
- Dwarf specimens
- Plants labelled at least two zones lower than the hardiness zone for your general area
- Plants with one or more coastal characteristics.

ALTERNATIVES TO BIG BOX GARDEN CENTRES

As you saw with my blueberry plant story, many factors can cause a healthy garden-centre plant to perish at the coast. Those three remaining tall blueberry bushes that narrowly escaped a fatal assault from the elements are now doing well in their new, protected location. But it was a slow recovery. I have learned the hard way. I now turn to the many other options that we have as gardeners. I would like to highlight a few here for you.

Recently, a dear neighbour who knew about my past issues with growing blueberries at the coast offered to dig up five of his low-growing blueberry plants for me to try out on the water side of our property. They experienced some leaf burn at first, but are vibrant and fruitful now. (And, yes, they turn crimson in the fall!) These plants were already acclimatized to seaside conditions and their short stature is most certainly an advantage at the coast.

Relocating plants that are already thriving in your general area is an excellent alternative to shopping for

Lowbush blueberries transplanted from a nearby property

Two gulls resting in the morning mist near native grasses on a coastal property

your gardening needs and interests. To learn how to do so, a good first step is to make connections with other coastal gardeners. Joining a local garden club is a good way to meet experienced gardeners and to find out about local growers and nurseries.

Maria Kuttner, a fellow gardener and member of our local gardening club, sings its praises as follows: "Gardening clubs like ours bring in local speakers, organize plant exchanges for members, and hold public plant sales. We sell plants that have spread beyond the capacity of our own gardens, thus ensuring that they are successfully grown in our zone. Every garden club normally has several expert gardeners who gladly give advice."

The guest speakers offer a range of angles on gardening. Some are simply highly dedicated and successful self-taught gardeners. Others are active or retired botanists with exceptional expertise to share. And, from time to time, a local nursery operator with specialized insight into our specific climactic conditions will give an informative talk.

There also are many choices for your garden above and beyond potted plants. Some plants can be started from bulbs, roots, or corms, which can be obtained from local seed-and-bulb catalogues. The same zone advice applies. Read the information well, as photos tend to be seductive. Mature specimens can be easily divided for propagation, while others, like privet, forsythia, and cotoneaster, for example, root so easily that placing a fresh cutting in good, moist soil will produce a new plant. These methods give way to plants that stand a much better chance at getting

Bulbs, roots, and corms are another way of introducing plants to the coastal garden.

established quickly and successfully at the coast, since the parent shrub is a locally grown plant.

Using native plants is another guaranteed successful way to create a vibrant, carefree garden (see chapter 5). Nevertheless, when it comes to growing garden plants well acclimatized to life by the sea, I am partial to starting from seed. It is one of my favourite ways to garden. Plants started indoors in late winter are a fresh reminder that spring renewal is soon approaching, while those started outdoors represent, to me, anticipation. The most exciting spring event is when the little seeds that I have started indoors or scattered outdoors eventually come up. For those willing to try, I have devoted the entire next chapter to my enthusiasm for starting from seed.

4

Starting from Seed at the Coast

I don't remember planting that.
—Denise Adams—

Finding a suitable quotation to open each chapter of the book was easy, until I got to this one. I couldn't for the life of me find one that worked. My husband's off-the-wall suggestion was for me to quote myself! So I asked him what he felt was my most famous garden saying.... It's true. I am continually mesmerized by what shows up on its own, even here by the sea. Plants appear in surprising, even unexpected places. Their chance at life is just that, a chance. A seed either falls in an inhospitable environment or a welcoming one. Many of my clients who are new to gardening by the sea quickly gain enough confidence in their knowledge and abilities to move on to something more adventurous. That is when I introduce them to growing plants for the coast from seed—my forte!

Growing from seed is a most gratifying method of gardening.

GROWING FROM SEED

I once read: "Real gardeners grow from seed." While an art in itself, growing plants from seed need not become a snooty ambition as the phrase suggests. Think of it as the simplest act of down-to-earth gardening.

Seeds are amazing. There isn't a more dramatic before-and-after effect than starting a plant from a seed! They are so tiny when compared to their parent. Some look like dust. They appear lifeless and insignificant, but given a bit of moisture, warmth, and sunlight, what began as a speck turns into a vigorous life form. If only we could see with the naked eye all of the biological activity that takes place from seed to sprout and from sprout to mature plant. Seeds are really miniscule little planets in dormancy. Once the process begins, a very complex network of interdependent organisms furiously get to work. A seed sprouting on an indoor windowsill while snow still flies represents hope. It is a reminder that winter is temporary—that life outside will become hospitable once again.

If planning to start from bought seed, take note of how the seeds are packaged. Unless tightly sealed,

Lemon grass started on a windowsill in February

I avoid buying seeds from outdoor nurseries because they are often exposed to damaging fluctuations in moisture. I have found that those ordered from catalogues are more reliable. If ordering seeds, be sure to use a locally based company, preferably one within or close to your province or state. Ideally, you want seeds from plants that are acclimatized to your weather conditions. Starting from seed is not only an excellent alternative to buying what I call "prefab plants to go," but is one of the most gratifying methods of gardening. Seedlings get accustomed to your seaside setting from the very start, whereas store-bought plants undergo a period of shock. There is a kind of "people-to-plant relationship" when growing from seed. Tending them is not a chore but becomes a little labour of love. As if these weren't enough reasons to start plants from seed, let us not forget that seeds also save dollars!

To pore over seed catalogues once the deep-freeze sets in is a pleasurable activity. I tend to order very early, just because I like to get acquainted with the little seeds in person—catalogues don't show us what they look like. I rarely buy transplants. I prefer to start plants from seed, some indoors and others outdoors. I enjoy watching the progress, especially of those begun indoors when it is still so cold outside. My list from seed catalogues is quite extensive, particularly for the vegetable garden. Although I collect most flower seeds myself, I always order a small repertoire of favourite flower seeds, and every year I try something new (see p. 140).

I have been growing from seed since I was a child. My father got me started when I was about five years old. He saved me the trouble of learning from trial and error, and I think my readers would appreciate the same benefit. The act of growing from seed is actually very simple. There are only a few issues to sort out.

Beginners may wonder which plants to start inside and which to direct seed outdoors. Some coastal gardeners may like to venture into collecting their own seeds from plants found thriving at the coast. And then there are the differences between annuals, biennials, and perennials. Some plants started from seed naturalize well and come back each year by self-seeding. These are annuals. Generally, though, the seeds of annual "garden" plants do not survive the winter; they have to be collected in the fall, stored, and then reseeded manually in the early spring in order to come back fresh. Seeds of biennial plants flower in their second year of growth. Then they die, leaving their seed behind to continue the cycle. As with annuals, some biennial plants self-seed, but most have to be started manually. Perennial plants are a little more complicated. These are plants that live several

Coastal Tip

The coastal climate has an affect on plant reproduction patterns and longevity. Some annuals can behave as biennials and some biennials can behave as perennials at the coast. Here, pansies, for example—usually considered annuals—can return year after year as a perennial would. Foxglove, a biennial, comes back the third year in my area, but is much shorter and more compact.

Foxglove growing among beach grass

years. They do not rely on seeds to come back or to reproduce. Although they produce seeds and can be started from them, it is usually more efficient to divide perennials by the roots or to start them from stem propagation.

STARTING SEEDS INDOORS

The point of starting seeds indoors is to have them mature faster than they would out in the cold spring soil. This means an earlier start and, as a result, a longer blooming period. Starting seeds indoors requires commitment, though. Unless you plan to use a grow light, you will have to chase sunny spots around the house. You will also have to ensure seeds have adequate moisture and gradually introduce the seedlings to coastal conditions before planting them permanently outdoors. This is called "hardening off" (see Coastal Tip, p. 50). I don't bother with grow lights because the only place I could fit one of these units would be on the kitchen table. Some fellow gardeners, however, could not imagine gardening life without their grow lights. They work well in the dimmest of basements. Plants need lights-out at night for about five hours; someone has to remember to flick the switch or set it up to turn off and on automatically.

The plants I start indoors tend to be shade- and partial-shade-loving plants. This eliminates the need to chase the sun as it moves around the house, a good south-facing windowsill will do. Another reason I prefer shade and partial-shade plants is that we get so much fog here at the coast. Sun-loving plants can experience light deprivation and as a result, produce fewer flowers with less vibrant colours. Watering seedlings is a crucial task. A lot can go wrong if not done carefully (see "Seedling Watering Tip," p. 49).

If I wish to have a lot of one plant, I grow it from seed. The impact of colour is always greatest when there is a lot of it. There is one little annual that is, to me, indispensable in the coastal garden: the lowly lobelia. "Crystal Palace" lobelia is a short variety with stunning cobalt blue flowers atop compact bronze-green foliage, colours that flow well with the seaside palette. It is a tiny but bushy little plant with stamina.

When started indoors, lobelia will bloom from mid-June until it succumbs to an episode of deep frost, late November to early December at the coast. These little gems are a great way to fill in blank areas between young foundation plants while waiting for them to mature. Lobelia comes in white, rose, violet, and various shades of blue. Its seeds, though miniscule, are relatively easy to start indoors as they are happy in partial shade. Once planted outside, you will soon discover that they thrive in cold, damp, foggy weather. No deadheading is required. They just keep going and going....

Tips for Sowing Tiny Seeds

Pour seeds onto a wide, white dinner plate. (If seeds are light in colour, use a dark plate so they stand out.) To spread seeds thinly over the soil, moisten the tip of your index finger with your breath then press it over the seeds on the plate. Gently rub your thumb and index finger together over the soil surface to drop seeds thinly and avoid overcrowding. Finally, press seeds firmly into the soil surface.

Starting Lobelia Indoors

Step 1: Fill seedling plugs (or any clean, perforated container) with light, moist potting soil mix—or even better, a seed-starter mix (some gardeners use flats with a depth of 3–4 cm [1 1/2 in.] of soil).

Seedling Watering Tip

Watering seedlings and transplants with a spout can be, to them, akin to a sudden monsoon. Their tender shoots and roots can be severely damaged. Instead, provide moisture by soaking the entire tray of plugs in a large casserole dish of water for just a few minutes. Rain- or snowmelt water is much better than treated water (which is high in sodium), and should be at room temperature. If only individual compartments need water, use a dropper or turkey baster.

Lobelia transplants soak up water from a casserole dish

Step 2: To keep roots moist and cool, line container holding plant pots or flat with a sheet of tinfoil, shiny side out, to deflect hot sun rays from roots.

Step 3: Sprinkle seeds lightly over soil containers. Press down firmly.

Step 4: Close with a clear cover, 2–4 cm (3/4–1 1/2 in.) above soil surface. If using plastic wrap, use tooth picks, blunt side up, to keep plastic above soil. Provide a good light source (south-facing window) and warmth (room temperature).

Step 5: Remove plastic cover gradually over three to four days, when most plants have more than two leaves. Keep soil moist—not wet.

Step 6: Where needed, thin plants to about 1 cm (1/2 in.) apart. (Tweezers are helpful; see p. 50)

Step 7: Harden off gradually. Transplant to the garden when all risk of frost has passed (see "Coastal Tip," p. 50).

Crystal Palace lobelia flowers

Thinning lobelia seeds with tweezers

Growing from seed indoors can be challenging when you're at work all day and your plants are left in a hot sunny window. That certainly was the case for me when I was teaching full-time. I worried that my plants would dry up before I got home. Blessed with a classroom featuring large south-facing windows, I decided to take my trays of bedding plants to work and leave them there from Monday to Friday to soak up the natural light. I was able to keep an eye on them and water as needed. This was a good workable arrangement.

One particular year, I decided to try growing dwarf cosmos for my seaside garden. When they got to be about 3 cm (1 1/4 in.) tall, there appeared to be two distinct varieties—similar in some ways, but completely different in others. This was quite puzzling, and it took me a while to figure it out. One of them had to be a "weed." You guessed it. A mystery student had taken advantage of my dedication to the plants by adding some of his/her cannabis seeds in there (or was it a joke?). Teachers beware.

Coastal Tip: Hardening off Indoor Plants for the Seaside Garden

- Young plants started indoors should have at least four true leaves (those that come after the first two baby leaves on new sprouts) before getting time outside.*
- Starting about two weeks before the last frost date, when the temperature is at least 15 degrees Celsius (60 degrees Fahrenheit), with no wind, begin introducing plants to the outdoors for no more than ten minutes at a time at first and in the shade (or they will fry!).**
- To acclimatize plants gently, gradually increase their time outside in ten-minute increments, exposing them ever so gently to direct sunlight. If you notice leaves blanching (turning pale), it has been too long. Sunlight intensity is magnified at the coast as it bounces off the water, sand, and rocks.
- Continue to increase time outside gradually. When transplants are able to stay out all day, you may begin leaving them out overnight.

*Always stay informed about the weather forecast. Early spring night frosts are common and fatal to seedlings. Find the last frost date for your area—this is when it is safe to transfer young plants to the garden (usually mid-June).

**You may begin the hardening off process earlier if weather permits.

Hardened-off lobelia, ready to be planted outside

FROM GERMINATION TO THE GROUND

There is another way to grow plants from seed indoors. This method requires no soil, but moves directly from germination to planting the little sprouts outside, once all danger of frost has passed. Timing is important, and this works best with "big" seeds. A larger annual I cannot imagine being without is the ever-flowering nasturtium. Gathering my own pea-sized nasturtium seeds has become a yearly fall ritual.

Unfortunately, there is no way to ensure flower colour when collecting your own seeds. At one time, I thought that seeds collected from yellow nasturtiums would sprout plants bearing yellow flowers, and seeds collected from ruby-red nasturtiums would yield ruby-red flowers. It turns out that this is not the case. Pollinators go from flower to flower indiscriminately. As a result, genetic information gets mixed up. Every nasturtium seed holds a surprise. Not to worry. Whatever the colour outcome, they are all on the warm side of the colour wheel (yellows/oranges/reds), or, in a visual gardener's terms, the "sunset" side. The warm colours of nasturtiums make them the ultimate plant for dramatically contrasting the cool colours of the Atlantic Ocean. If I could ever get a dream job, it would be to name plant varieties. Since these are my own homegrown specimens, I have taken the liberty of naming my nasturtiums (see p. 53).

One might wonder how nasturtiums, with their trailing habit, survive the fierce winds and salt spray of coastal areas. For one, the seaside climate keeps them rather compact; the cool breezes stunt their growth somewhat and force the plants into a bushy form rather than allowing them to sprawl out. Furthermore, the stems are succulent (with rubbery, moisture-retaining properties), which helps them withstand scorching winds surprisingly well. Also, in my case, their resilience can be attributed to the fact that they were grown from seeds collected from the most vibrant and healthy plants nearest the water's edge.

I prefer to germinate nasturtium seeds indoors in a container rather than plant them directly into the ground. This way I ***know*** that what has been planted will take. Not all collected seeds germinate. Germination is a bit erratic, but it usually begins after about one week indoors. I start germination in early June so nasturtiums can be planted in the middle of the month, when all threat of frost has passed.

How to Germinate Nasturtiums

- Begin collecting mature seeds (those that have fallen off the plant) in early fall from the most robust plants, especially from the healthiest plants closest to the water. Wash seeds well with a bit of dish soap in cold water. Once dry, place seeds in a paper bag or small cardboard box.
- Overwinter seeds indoors in a cool, dark, dry place. A closet or drawer will do just fine.
- Come spring, about one week before the last frost date, remove seeds and wash again in cold, soapy water.
- Place seeds on damp paper towel in a lidded container. Place container in a dark spot that you are

Nasturtium seeds are mature when the plant drops them, mid-fall.

Rinse seeds well for storage and again before germinating

Keep seeds on dampened paper towel in a covered container

sure to check often: in the pantry, in the microwave oven, or on the shower floor, for example.

- As soon as you see a seed begin to sprout, place it outside in cultivated soil just deep enough to cover it, with the root pointing down. Mark the seed with a toothpick if its leaves are not yet visible, to avoid "double planting."

One morning, a neighbour came up the driveway to speak to my husband, Rick. But something captured his attention. The cascading multicoloured nasturtiums that I grew from seed were at their peak of performance. The neighbour seemed awestruck. He asked Rick what that was growing in the stone bank. Rick answered flippantly: "I have no idea...some kind of flower. All I know about flowers is that it is something you give the wife when you've been bad." I had quite a chuckle over his spontaneous response. I immediately shouted: "That one is for the book!"

ABOUT COLLECTING YOUR OWN SEEDS

To ensure good germination, seeds must be mature. Take time to observe the method of dispersal for plants of interest. Generally, seeds are fully mature when the plant drops them.

When seeds have opened and put out a root, they are ready to plant.

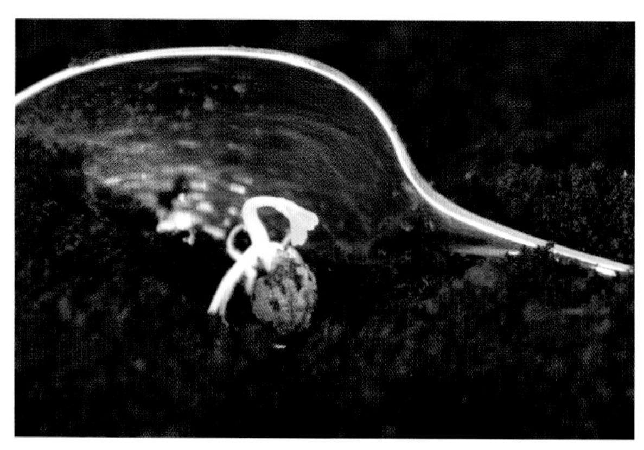

A germinated nasturtium seed gets planted in garden soil

The many faces of nasturtium: (clockwise from top left) "Orange Alert," "Marmalade," "Rosy Cheeks", and "Lemon Meringue"

Plants have various methods of dispersing their offspring. If the seed is contained in a seedpod, wait until the plant begins to release them. The seeds should rattle when you shake the pod. Some pods, like those of the beach pea, split open to drop their seeds. Others, like those of campion and poppies, will form exit holes as they dry up, allowing seeds to fall through. The seeds of most flowering plants can be found atop the centre of the spent flower. Some have little makeshift parachutes similar to dandelion seeds. These seeds can be carried long distances from the parent plant. A rare few, including impatiens and balsam, have a spring mechanism that can catapult their seeds away from the parent's footing. Unsuspecting visitors and children are surprised and amused when I ask them to touch these swollen seedpods.

Close-up of a balsam bloom with seedpods

Plants that fling their seeds can be challenging to capture. The best way is to bend the seedpod-laden stems gently toward an open bucket and then shake briskly. It's a hit-or-miss exercise.

> **COASTAL TIP**
>
> A seed has as distinct a face as its flower. Experienced seed collectors can tell what plant a seed or its pod belongs to simply by looking at its shape, size, and colour.

COLLECTING AND STORING SEEDS BY THE SEA

Any attractive seed-bearing plant at the coast is worth considering for the seaside garden. Some may be natives, like beach pea, fireweed, and bindweed; others may be naturalized garden escapees like lupin, purple asters, black-eyed Susans, wild chicory, or tall phlox (also known as sweet rocket). Seeds collected from plants that grow successfully at the coast will ensure the hardiness of the next crop.

Collecting seeds from natural settings is a bit magical. It is like playing Mother Nature. All that is needed is to cast them where you would like them

(Top) Forget-me-not; (bottom) black-eyed Susans

to come up. The best time is in April, when storm surges are less likely. Watch for flowering to end, collect seeds in a bucket or paper bag, and then place it in an unheated shed or garage over winter. This allows them to experience freezing as they would in nature but without the damaging effects of repeated wet and dry events. Some seeds should not be left where they are accessible to rodents. I have learned that squirrels steal and store coriander and poppy seedpods.

I always collect many more seeds than I can use. I cast them where I would like to see them come up—along roadsides, meadows, or at water's edge—and give the rest away. Sharing seeds is gratifying, and appreciated by those who receive them.

Come spring, scratch the ground surface to give seeds an advantage to germinate and set roots before

Coastal Tip

As much as possible, collect seeds from plants that are closest to the water's edge. These are more likely to produce plants with a tolerance to coastal conditions than seeds taken from protected inland plants.

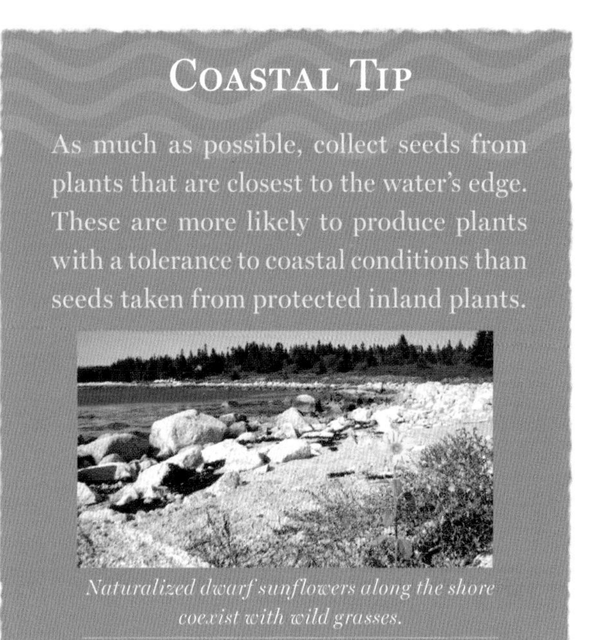

Naturalized dwarf sunflowers along the shore coexist with wild grasses.

Wild chicory

Purple asters

Fireweed

Seaside Suggestion

Beach pea seeds are easy to collect and make a great ground cover at the coast wherever you cast them. Their blooms are smaller but just as elegant as old-fashioned sweet peas, and their fruit just as delicious and nutritious as garden-variety peas! For a novel side dish, collect the little green peas as soon as pods form and swell, then steam and serve them as you would regular garden peas.

Beach pea blossoms

Last year's campion, a biennial, is ready to be moved from a row in the vegetable garden to a prepared spot in the yard.

strong winds blow them off course. Enjoy the summer show and continue the cycle of seed collecting all over again in the fall. At the end of the season, it can be a bit tricky to find the seeds of plants you hope to bring into the coastal garden, so I have taken photos of my favourites to help you identify them (see p. 56)

PLANTING SEEDS DIRECTLY OUTDOORS

Direct seeding garden annuals outdoors at the coast requires a lot of patience. They can get washed away by hard rains, eaten by birds or rodents, and germination is oh...so...slow. Furthermore, native vegetation begins to settle in and seedlings are often unable to compete. This is why native and naturalized annuals are your best bet for direct seeding.

Biennials and perennials are a much better way to achieving success with planting directly outdoors. A great strategy for ensuring hardy seaside plants is to start biennial and perennial plants from seed in a more protected part of your coastal property. I have gotten in the habit of keeping a row free in my vegetable garden for starting favourite biennials like campion, money plant, and columbine, and another row for new perennials. The reason I start biennials and perennials in the protection of the vegetable garden is twofold: First, they have no visual appeal

Beach pea is a prolific native coastal plant.

Beach pea seeds are easy to collect and will grow wherever you drop them in the seaside garden. Consider it for a dense ground cover.

the first year. Second, the young plants could get lost among other plants, get crowded out, or get mistaken for a weed. The following year, they will have developed into strong transplants that are better able to withstand the elements. These are then ready to set flowers in a spot specially prepared for them, where they can be enjoyed as part of the overall coastal garden experience.

Starting from seed is an approach that requires a wholehearted interest and hands-on involvement in gardening. You will feel all the more connected with the wonders of nature and, in some small way, know that you had a hand in its creation from the ground up. How gratifying. A word of caution though: once you achieve success with growing from seed, it can become an obsession. Your house will end up looking

Used facial tissue boxes make great seed organizers.

like mine: seeds stored in every closet, drawer, cupboard—even the refrigerator. Late winter and early spring, every sunny windowsill will become covered in pots and seed trays. Family members and friends begin to feel that you give more attention to your seedlings than to them. But once everything is blooming gloriously outside, they will forget.

5

Easy-Care "Seaworthy" Gardens

A weed is a plant that has mastered every survival skill
except for learning to grow in rows.
—Doug Larson—

The greatest lesson in gardening for those new to it, is that it evolves. What we plant today is not static; there will be changes in width, height, and shape. Young perennials give way to weeds at first, but once they fill out, uninvited guests get choked out. There may come a stage in a prized plant's life when it has become too wide or too tall and must be cut back or relocated. Gardening is as cyclical and as dynamic as raising a family. Expect change and pick your battles.

Later on, in chapter 11, "Let the Sea Steal the Show," I make the case that at the coast, we can get away with being very casual about "weeds" in the garden. Allowing native vegetation to coexist with garden favourites here and there may not be acceptable in some settings, as in publicly funded gardens, for instance.

A coastal property with uninterrupted majestic views, left natural

A city garden and country garden conjure up images of two very different styles. We think of a "city garden" as relatively small and formal with crisp edges, composed of mostly exotic or novelty plants. We think of a country garden as a well cared for but less defined space, made mostly of fruit trees, heritage shrubs, flowers, vines, and herbs.

There are many "garden styles": Victorian, medieval, Shakespearean, Tudor, knot, topiary, traditional English.... Maintaining a certain style can mean a lot of work. We are fortunate that by the sea, there are no such expectations. We can keep gardening life simple. This chapter offers simple suggestions that will help keep a casual garden from getting out of hand. These basic tips apply to all garden styles, but seaside gardeners really deserve a break: we have the untamed coastal climate to contend with. This environment can be perilous to all but the hardiest plants.

TIPS AND TRICKS TO SAVE TIME AND WORK

Many of one kind

If you like a certain flower and know you can grow it well, plant lots of it. There are several advantages to planting generous amounts of one kind:

Sea thrifts

they all bloom at the same time, so the impact of colour will be strong, they have the same sun/shade requirements, and they won't compete with taller plants or drown out shorter ones. Together, they are stronger. When onshore winds hit, there is safety in numbers. If instead you plant one of everything that you like in an area of the yard, you'll end up with a circus. Furthermore, favourites can quickly lose their "identity" in a crowd of individuals. Each plant will have different needs and life phases, and this can easily become overwhelming. Caring for many individuals is far more complicated than tending to a group of one kind in an appointed area.

Bird nest spruce, creeping juniper, and contoneaster flow easily over bedrock

Spreading and creeping varieties

Have lots of ground cover. Short plants with a sprawling habit are fast growing and inhibit weed growth. These days, the choices are remarkable. Several standard specimens have been bred to produce yellow, red, and variegated foliage. Many dwarf conifers, like juniper, cedar, cypress, and spruce, come in brilliant hues ranging from yellow to blue. If you are so fortunate to have elevations, indulge in plants with a cascading effect like cotoneasters, creeping Jenny, thyme, and clustering succulents. Robust vines like honeysuckle, hops, Virginia creeper, Boston ivy, and clematis are all showy, carefree plants that conceal less desirable vegetation. No weeding necessary. Spreading and creeping varieties need no winter protection, provided that they are specimens hardy to zone 4 or lower.

Siberian bellflower spills over piled flagstone, met with spreading native ferns

Plant at arm's length

In order to tend to your plants in comfort, without fear of trampling over anything of value or harming your back, you need to be able to access all parts of the garden patch easily. Having raised beds is a great back-saver. If you want a large swath of plants in one area, leave a path the width of a mower or tiller for yourself. Use stepping stones, a thick mulch, pine needles, or mowed grass for low-maintenance access. A spiral path to the centre or a loop with an entrance and exit will grant easy passage. Incorporate little places to sit long enough to relax, observe, hear, smell, and touch, and feel grateful to experience the wonders of this blue and green planet.

Create Curves

When putting in a garden bed, keep the spirit of the sea in mind. Undulating lines, like those of the shore, inspire contemplation. Circles and ovals, half moons, kidney shapes, and other irregular organic shapes are

Curves are so much more appealing than straight lines.

reminiscent of an oasis. Brisk winds are set off course when they encounter a curve, whereas they tend to slam into a straight formation, causing more damage. Unlike square and rectangular beds, curved flower beds can take a few imperfections without appearing neglected. You won't feel called to sharpen the edges of the garden patch quite as often, just one good spring cleanup will do.

Plant in Layers of Height

The effect of hills and dunes is more interesting than a flat surface. If the flower garden is an "island" in the lawn, plant tall specimens at the centre and then shorter to shortest from there. If the garden is against a structure like a shed, again, plant tall at the back and shortest at the front. These two strategies make the garden look full-bodied, especially if composed of plants with various blooming times. Only the tallest weeds will get your attention. Pull them out and relax about the rest. Your plants will also benefit from not having to compete for light when planted this way. Three varieties per garden patch will suffice: a June, a July, and an August bloomer, for example. As long as something is in bloom, faded plants will go unnoticed and you can tend to spent blooms when convenient.

WEED-SUPPRESSION TRICKS

In cases where it is important to keep native vegetation out or "weeds" down, the recommendation is usually to use landscaping fabric. But it has limitations and can give the gardener a false sense of security. It is not a permanent solution to weeding. Invaders will eventually sneak through and spit their offspring all over the mulch before you get a handle on their seed production. Furthermore, brisk winds and rain often wash the mulch off the slippery, unsightly cloth surface. Another annoyance is that annuals cannot be

Layering plants from short to tall holds interest and creates drama.

Use flowers as weed suppressant: where they come up, a weed cannot.

added to fill in between perennials while they mature. The young garden looks sparse and polka dot–like. I would sooner have more flowers than stretches of dead, empty space.

A good alternative to landscaping cloth is to fill in the blanks of your garden with a broadleaf plant, like lady's mantel, nasturtiums, even salad greens or low-growing herbs, that will starve weeds of light. I have found that planting nasturtiums between perennials serves this purpose particularly well for the added colour (see p. 53). The sea keeps nasturtiums small, and when stressed by wind or overcrowding, they bloom profusely. We usually think of honeysuckle as a climbing plant, but left alone it makes great a filler, ground cover, and weed barrier. And the long-lasting blossoms and fragrance are quite lovely.

Another trick is to cast seeds from an easy favourite annual, like Johnny jump ups, dwarf flax, lobelia, or feverfew, between the perennials. Where they come up, a weed cannot. And if one does, it is usually stunted or unnoticeable. If a weed does become visible, it gets my attention and is plucked immediately as I do my leisurely rounds. So no fabric for me, except directly under a prized perennial until it becomes established.

I do like a layer of black mulch over the entire bed to make the colours stand out. Mulching without landscape fabric allows other choice plants to grow through and coexist with foundation plants. If your waterfront is blessed with deposits of seaweed, consider drying and shredding it to use as mulch. Be sure to collect only rain-rinsed seaweed or the salt will eventually weaken the plants. (See chapter 8 for more on seaweed).

ABOUT THAT "PERFECT" TURF

Dare to be different at the coast. Really, the point of having lawn is for easy walking. That's it. We have an obsession with "perfect turf" in this part of the world, but keeping a monocultural lawn requires a great deal of effort, time, and cost. Furthermore, few of us give much thought to its toll on the environment, especially at the coast. Keeping a "weedless" lawn results in intensive use of fertilizers, herbicides, lime applications, chemical runoff, fuel, carbon emissions, thatching, aeration, greenhouse gasses from mowing and irrigation, not to mention noise pollution from the need to mow frequently.

Well, the Newfies on my husband's side have a solution to every problem. Have you heard this one?

A Newfoundlander mowing his lawn noticed a truckload of sod drive down his street. The Newfie stopped what he was doing and scratched his head.

"What's you tinkin' Garge?" asked his neighbour.

"Bys-o-bys" George says. "If I ever wins da lottery, dat's what I'm gonna do."

"What's dat, me son?" asks the neighbour.

"I'm gonna get me lawn hauled away, just like dat, to be mowed."

I hesitate to state this sad truth, but mowing the lawn is likely the only experience most people have with gardening. When it comes to lawn, less is best. If we could live with a mixed turf, as does Mr. Elwood

Mr. Elwood's lawn lets the sea steal the show.

at his spectacular seaside setting (p. 66), the environment would be better off. His would be considered a weedy lawn by most standards. It is comprised of several short, wild plants and mosses along with naturally low-growing native grasses and lovely buttercups. Mr. Elwood does not add fertilizers or lime to the walking areas; this green turf is completely left in nature's hands. The breathtaking views of his oceanfront lot override any criticisms one may have about the quality of his lawn. It is mowed no more than two or three times a season and its coarse texture is perfectly acceptable for walking. The added benefit is that dandelions—the bane of homeowners—cannot get established, the native soil is too acidic.

RELOCATING LITTLE SEASIDE GEMS

More shows up in the garden than what I have purposely sown. Volunteer plants are often garden escapees that pop up here and there, but not necessarily where planned. I am speaking about naturalized garden plants that have reseeded themselves in new parts of the yard on their own. You will soon discover that seeds travel at the coast. Onshore winds inadvertently move seeds to unexpected places, the driveway, the vegetable garden, under a shrub or two.... Pretty flowers are always a pleasant sight, even when they show up in an odd spot. Consider them a freebie that can be moved to a new location. My neighbour was delighted when one of my favourites showed up in her dog's large outdoor pen. She scooped up the cluster

Daisies relocated at the shore

of blue forget-me-nots with a little spade and moved them to her front step, where they could be better appreciated.

The plants I am referring to are generally self-seeding annuals or biennials. Good examples of such flexible plants are: forget-me-not, foxglove, daisies, Johnny jump ups, various pansies and violas, tall phlox, mallow, black-eyed Susans, sea holly, feverfew, and lupins to name a few. Since they have acclimatized to coastal living, they are quite tough. A crude scoop of a trowel will do the trick. My motto is: if they grew here effortlessly, they can be relocated effortlessly. Relocation is easier on these plants before they go into bloom, but I have had success moving self-seeded plants around even at that "high-need" time of their life cycle. It is always easier on a plant to be moved early in its life. Get to know the plants you appreciate by their early foliage and move them as soon as you spot them. To do it on a drizzly or overcast day certainly helps reduce the stress of relocation.

I often move plants to new locations where they can be better appreciated. These found plants are, to me, a gift. I cannot discard a perfectly healthy, living plant that makes a pretty flower. I would rather give it away if no space can be found for it. What can't be adopted often forces me to start another flower bed in an otherwise dull part of the yard. And more flowering plants mean less lawn to mow.

Garden phlox grow in the protection of native plants and trees

This little gem is a bluebead lily. A native of coastal forests—but not unique to it—its flower is a miniature yellow lily. For dazzling flecks of naturalized blue by the sea, it is easily transplanted to a north side of a coastal property in early spring.

INTRODUCING NATIVE PLANTS

More and more native Maritime plants are appearing in garden centres these days. They are gaining popularity because they are hardier than many exotics and are consistent with the natural scenery. The choices, however, are limited. Local growers may know of private gardeners with a special interest in propagating particular native plants.

Moving plants from the wild to a coastal garden is a viable alternative. But it is important to be mindful of the fact that there are sensitive ecosystems along the coast. Never disturb vegetation in pristine or botanically unique coastal areas. Rather, look along ditches and roadsides by the sea. Plants are opportunistic. Given a chance, coastal trees and shrubs do settle successfully in accessible locations where there is less competition.

It is ***always*** a good idea to ask before digging. In all my experiences, residents were quite flattered that I had seen something of value in what to them was a nearby "wasteland." They are especially impressed when I assure them that I will be careful to infill the spot where I have dug. Surrounding natural materials like rocks, moss, and plant debris serve as adequate fillers. Transplanting is best done in early spring while the plant is still dormant—before the month of May. During a summer coastal drive with my family, I came across a large colony of native blue flag irises growing happily in a roadside ditch. I took note of where they were growing and retuned the following spring to dig a few up, keeping in mind to leave enough to allow the plant to fill out again and keep going. These native irises are a spectacular sight in mass-bloom.

When digging up native plants for the coastal garden, choose young, robust specimens whose size you can manage. Younger and smaller are better. When it comes to shrubs and young trees, a general guideline to remember is that the root ball is about the same size as the plant itself. If the plant is the size of a footstool, the root ball will be as well—for me, far too large and heavy to transport. Know your level of strength.

Coastal Tip

Now and then, I come across a freshly fallen tree in a coastal forest. The uprooted area often has pulled out surrounding younger trees along with it. No digging required. Simply tug at the plant until it loosens, root ball intact. You now have a free, ready-to-plant beauty.

A young spruce uprooted by a fallen tree

The easiest native plants to introduce to the coastal garden are those found growing on top of boulders. This is not an uncommon sight in moist maritime climates. Many ground covers—ferns, shrubs, and even stunted trees—live a precarious existence in such locations. While accustomed to stress, these plants gratefully move to a new, more fertile spot. Their foundation can be peeled off almost as easily as a mat off the floor! Roll it up and take it home to the seaside garden. Be sensitive to the plant's light requirements, and find a spot of the garden that closely matches its previous home.

step 1

step 2

step 3

Conifers enjoy new more promising location.

In the fall, a native bayberry shrub gets a spade cut in preparation for a spring move.

TRANSPLANTING NATIVE TREES AND SHRUBS

Step 1: Look for a plant living in a habitat similar to where you plan to move it. Shrubs should be no taller than knee-high. Young trees should be no taller than hip-high with a caliper size (trunk width) of no more than 1–2 cm (1/3–3/4 in.). Take into account light requirements. Mark it with a painted stake or ribbon.

Step 2: Return to the marked plant early to mid-fall. Push a spade in about 30 cm (1 ft.) away from the main stem. Cut all around the root ball. This will allow the severed roots time to heal and form a condensed root ball for easy transfer in the spring.

Step 3: The following spring, as soon as the ground has thawed, dig the plant out. Fill a bucket with some of the surrounding soil. Infill the hole with natural material, i.e. rocks, moss, rotted wood, etc., taken from the area.

Step 4: Make the new hole in your garden twice the size of the root ball. Mix the plant's original soil with new soil and a heaping handful of bone meal. Add water.

Step 5: Lower the root ball into the wet soil mixture. Press down firmly. Infill the ground around the plant with the remaining mixture of original and local soil. Water generously.

Care: the first year, keep the plant well watered and spray down with fresh water following strong winds to keep salt off. Once established, it will take care of itself.

A SWELL THOUGHT: FOUR SEASIDE FAVOURITES

To wrap up this chapter, I would like to introduce you to four seaside winners that cohabitate with native coastal vegetation wonderfully. I call them "Seaside Pink Perfections." They are very showy at the coast and require absolutely no care.

A lovely plant that has followed me from my first coastal garden in Boutiliers Point is number one on this list. Since I did not know its identity or common name at the time, I baptized it "Larsen's pinks" (explanation to follow). To keep referring to these spectacular little plants as simply "those" over and over was as dignified as the name Buddy Wasisname and the Other Fellers (a band from Newfoundland). I had to give this plant a name that I could hang on to for identification.

This lovely flowering annual, which, at the coast, behaves more as a biennial, shows up in my garden on its own every year. When I first discovered it, Mr. Larsen, my next-door neighbour at the time, had some too. He believed that they might have come from a package of wildflower seeds he had spread, but did not know the plant's identity. I recently contacted a botanist who identified it as either ***Silene armeria*** (Sweet William catchfly), or ***Silene colorata*** (pink catchfly). I was puzzled by the reference to a "fly-catching" plant. My initial thought was: this is not a carnivorous plant nor does it particularly attract insects....

Pink catchfly

Common plant names are much like surnames. They may seem arbitrary but they can all be traced back to the attributes of a distant relative. I have since discovered that this little "Seaside Pink Perfection" is related to a group of flowers bearing the name "catchfly" that secrete a sticky substance to trap meandering insects. One online source remarked that the remaining dead insects served to put off predatory bugs that might want to eat the plant. So for those to whom I have been giving seeds for pink catchfly since the early 1990s, it is now locally known as "Larsen's pinks"! Oops... It will be interesting to see if the name sticks now that it's original name has been discovered.

Pink catchfly is a relatively short (20–30 cm [8 in.–1 ft.]), loosely compact flowering plant with mint-green, semi-succulent leaves and stems. Since these are coastal characteristics, it should be no wonder it does so well at the coast. Although it self-seeds, its seeds are also easy to collect once the flowers have faded. Simply cast them where you would like to see clusters of vibrant hot-pink colour the following year. It blooms from mid-June to late September.

Perennial sweet pea is extremely robust despite its delicate appearance. As with its cousin, the garden

Pink catchfly is an easy, eye-catching plant for the coast.

Perennial sweet pea

Crown vetch is a strong guard against erosion.

sweet pea, it clings to whatever it can with its curling tendrils. These I purchased out of curiosity from a seed catalogue. I started them from seed, indoors, in April, then moved them to various parts of the garden and even down to the shore. To my great delight, they have been coming back year after year among native brambles and beach grasses. The perennial sweet pea is a fantastic July and August bloomer.

Crown vetch, though a paler pink, is similar to perennial sweet pea in that it, too, clings to other plants in order to keep its head up and catch sunlight. I dug some up from a ditch one early spring just after they had emerged from the ground. I then relocated them to a bank overlooking the sea. The plant now thrives among native vegetation and, in turn, anchors the slope against erosion. Crown vetch is an attractive plant for areas where mowing is impossible and where erosion is a constant concern.

Campion is a great performer at the coast. It comes in white and pale pink, but fuchsia is by far the showiest of all in the coastal garden. Since campion is a biennial that self-seeds easily, its standout

Pink campion has several coastal characteristics.

silvery foliage is best kept away from lawns. A good safeguard is to cut off the stems as soon as the flowers have faded, before they get a chance to turn to seed. Back to coastal characteristics, I suspect the reason this plant does so well by the sea is that its leaves and stems are minty-green—a colour that deflects intense sunlight—and velvety, a coating that protects against direct stabs of salt from salt spray.

ROPE DRY... SUN
ROPE WET... RAIN
ROPE PALE... FOG
ROPE WHITE... SNOW
ROPE GONE...HURRICANE

6

Don't Give Up the Ship

Climate is what we expect, weather is what we get.
—Mark Twain—

Although frightful at times, the weather at the coast is by no means prohibitive to gardening. Most days, high winds last only for a short period, usually between 11 A.M. and 2 P.M., when warming air mixes with the cold surface of the sea. For all of our complaining about the weather in the Maritimes, we seaside gardeners do enjoy some perks at the coast.

The growing season by the sea actually outlives that of the inland, at least in Nova Scotia. Frost is delayed until late November, some years well into December. The ground doesn't freeze significantly until mid-January. We have less snow to shovel, if any. Some gardeners claim that the salty marine air acts as an antiseptic that wards off plant fungal disease. I for one can attest to this. I have not encountered here the mold-based plant infections that some inland gardeners endure. But the best news about coastal gardening is that we experience a much-reduced population of mosquitoes and blackflies. They seem to have an aversion to fog and salty air; the slightest onshore breeze disperses them. Another benefit is that coastal gardens tend to be far removed from monocultural landscapes, which breed bugs who specialize at sapping the life out of certain cultivars. We don't get such pests as potato beetles, cutworms, or army worms at the coast. These advantages are the envy of inland gardeners.

Growing at the coast, however, can test the most experienced of gardeners. The greatest challenge to growing a seaside garden is twofold: soil quality and exposure to the elements. While we can do something about soil quality (see next chapter), we have no control over the coastal climate. We have to live with it, make the best of it and, however possible, find ways around it. Each season has its challenges, but keep an open mind. There will be a few irritants to having a garden by the sea. High winds and salt spray are inevitable. You will, at times, find your flowers and leaves a little weathered looking, but they will survive. It is something like when you get to be a half-century old. On my big day, I looked to my spouse and said, "Honey, I am fifty now. Like my seaside garden, I too am entitled to a few physical flaws." Here is what can be expected of coastal climactic conditions in each season, and how the seaside gardener can overcome adversity and not "give up the ship."

Katie the lab, in a sou'wester, lives on Peggys Cove Road.

GARDENING AT THE COAST IN A FOUR-SEASON CLIMATE

COASTAL SPRING CLIMATE

Searing, chilly winds, sudden frost, dense fog, heavy rains, and wet flurries are the hallmark of spring by the sea in northern coastal climates, particularly during the months of March and early April. Now and then, however, we get teased by lovely mild, sunny days. Lobster fishers appreciate a break in the weather. These are also the days coastal gardeners can take advantage of. Early spring is absolutely the best time to start a coastal garden. Planting early allows more time for new young plants to get established before autumn storms hit. New plants need lots of time to build strong roots and energy reserves to get through Atlantic winter storms.

If you wish to introduce a native plant to your property or would like to relocate a favourite, the best time to do so is during its late-winter dormancy. Plants at that phase can weather mild frost without difficulty. This is actually an easier transition for a plant to make than later on, when they begin to put out new root growth that could potentially become damaged during transplantation.

Where you place your gardens in relation to the sea also makes a big difference for plant survival. The thing to keep foremost in mind is the direction of predominant winds. In my case, the fiercest winds come

Yellow mums get windswept even in the shelter of a shed

from the southwest. Nova Scotia's South Shore fisher folk call their waterproof head cover a "sou'wester" for that very reason. Shrubs and flowering perennials, when well chosen (see pp. 35–39), are quite forgiving, but in their first year of growth by the sea they need all the help they can get. Start them young and provide winter protection during their first year if they possess a cold-hardiness higher than zone 4 (see "Zone it Down" p. 39). Once established and acclimatized to their new surroundings, perennials should be able to take care of themselves.

Goldfish keep mosquito larvae out of rainwater, add a little interest to the yard, and you can bring them in for the winter.

COASTAL SUMMER CLIMATE

Summer by the sea is spectacular: not too cold, not too hot. But ocean-borne winds can be just as

Seaside Solution: Injured Birds

The migratory path of many birds follows the coast. It is always disheartening when a bird mistakes the reflection in a window for sea and sky. Here's how to deal with an injured bird.

As soon as a bird hits the window, go looking for it. Do not assume that it is dead, even if it isn't moving.

Quickly cover the bird without disturbing it, using a box or a large, opaque mixing bowl. Leave it covered for at least two hours. Allow just enough space for air to circulate from below. Unless you can hear the bird jumping around, do not check on it until the two hours are up. This period of undisturbed darkness will allow a bird in shock to rest, recover, and feel safe from predators. Chances are very good that your feathered friend will be able to fly off in gratitude.

After the two hours, lift the shelter slowly. Remain at a distance while the bird's eyes adjust to the light. If it doesn't fly off within ten minutes, take it to a safe place: under a crate or laundry basket with good-sized exit holes that will allow the bird to leave safely when it is ready. An old lobster trap also works well.

Give yourself a pat on the shoulder for a job well done when the little bird suddenly takes flight.

Place a large, opaque bowl over injured bird

Recovered bird is weak but is well enough to perch until strong enough to fly off

inhospitable to both garden and gardener. We suffer the same discomforts. When flower petals and foliage take flight, so does my sun hat. Fluid from my watery eyes and nose take a horizontal course and my cheeks endure a lashing from loose strands of hair. Forceful winds can persist for three to four days at a time at the coast, and salt spray can be potentially fatal to non-native plants. During these spells, the garden, the crashing waves, and the thunderous sound of pounding surf are best enjoyed from indoors. We aren't the only ones to suffer high winds: birds get off course. Not only that, but our seaside windows can potentially be fatal to them.

As soon as the wind calms down enough to go outside, get the hose out and give your plants a good spray of fresh water to wash off salt. It is not unusual for the seaside garden to experience episodes of drought during the height of gardening season.

Keep a source of fresh water at ground level. You may not get to see them, but coastal creatures will take advantage of it.

August tends to have the least amount of rainfall. Animals in the coastal forest can be hard-pressed to find a drink of fresh water. I was lucky to get a shot of this desperate snowshoe hair that came for a drink on a few occasions during a dry spell.

Many seaside homes have water treatment systems for their well water. But water softeners are typically treated with salt, and the last thing your seaside plants need is a drink of salty water. Treated water, much less salty than seawater, is fine to wash salt spray off plants, but should not be used to water them. Keep several rain collection barrels and check them often for mosquito larvae. Small tubs are easily emptied to prevent the insect from coming to term. I keep a couple of goldfish in the water collection tub to take care of mosquito larvae and any other buggy things that fall in (see p. 79).

COASTAL FALL CLIMATE

Autumn days at the shore are lovely and refreshing. I like to keep lawn furniture out as long as I can to enjoy the seaside garden and water views. However, fall is also hurricane season. Seaside gardeners would be wise to stay informed of the weather forecast this time of year. Tropical storms can intensify quickly, and fierce winds can hit suddenly and unannounced. It doesn't take much of a wind to topple a lawn chair and blow it into prized flowering plants and shrubs—or into a window! I have woken up several times to find a lawn chair or two floating at sea. Now, as a precaution, I keep my outdoor furniture secured at all times by tying them down to a fixed object. Other homeowners prefer to batten down the hatches only when a storm is in the forecast, but predictions are not always accurate. It's no fun moving all freestanding

Late summer to late fall is hurricane and tropical storm season. Notice the hail pellets on the ground.

items to a sheltered area when weather threatens in the middle of the night.

The sea has been known to form a fist of great force. Some seaside properties are susceptible to storm surges. Hurricanes and tropical storms often cause higher than usual tides that can spill over into our yards and gardens. Flood-prone areas are never suitable for growing perennials. Annual flowers, however, are less of a disappointment when destroyed by fall storms: their short life is about to end anyway, with the onset of winter. The most storm-tolerant plants at water's edge are native coastal plants. These serve as a natural green buffer—keep them! Add local cultural items such as driftwood, buoys, and retired lobster traps to add interest to these untamed areas.

Every year, tall, mature spruce trees are lost to stormy weather on our property. So I make sure to keep the tops of spruce that are within reach clipped. Trees growing close to one another should be thinned out to allow them to fill out rather than spurt up tall and scrawny. Also keep in mind that strong winds can crack stems and branches, subjecting a tree to disease and eventually, death. Always do an inspection following a storm to catch injuries early, before disease and insects set in. A good clean cut with a set of loppers will accelerate the wound's healing.

A lawn chair is secured to a post using strong rope

In September 2003, the storm of the century hit the Maritimes. Hurricane Juan carved a path of destruction along the coast of Nova Scotia, into Halifax, and throughout several inland areas. Coastal folks emerged trembling and sleepless the following morning to find wharves, fish stores, and roads completely washed out. In most places, electricity was out for an entire week.

Seaside Solution: Large Broken Tree Limbs

Paint is applied to a severed tree limb

As soon as a broken branch is discovered—if it appears to be beyond repair—sever it completely and snip off the shredded end to make a clean, angled cut. This will make it easier for the branch to heal over. For larger broken limbs, make a clean cut with a chainsaw and then cover the injury with an oil-based paint to prevent sap loss. If the injury is a fairly clean snap that can be pressed back into place, luck may be on your side. Wrap the joint tightly in duct tape. A piece of twine will also help keep the limb in place. The tree will be able to mend itself well within a year.

Seaside Suggestion

A preventative measure to tree limb breakage is to prune some of the branches out, allowing the wind to blow through with less resistance. Where winds are persistent, trees and shrubs are prone to developing a permanent lean. Planting them against a large, heavy item like a boulder will prevent this. It also will give roots a strong anchor around which to cling, to avoid wind and frost heave. Never plant something by the sea in the fall, it won't have sufficient time to get established or build resistance to the coastal climate.

A moose appears disoriented the day after a hurricane

Animals were confused. There were many sightings of shorebirds foreign to Nova Scotia: pelicans, laughing gulls, Bonaparte gulls, and kittiwakes. Mats of thick coastal vegetation—shrubs and old-growth coastal forest trees—were left flipped over like an old rug. The shore in Boutiliers Point, where my family lived at the time, was littered with everything imaginable: toys, a busted picnic table, the bow of a wooden boat, a shed rooftop, and truckloads of seaweed tangled in floating trees. The coast was a mess of exposed roots from uprooted trees. We thought it would take decades for shore vegetation to recover. But just a year later, what had appeared to be irreparable damage to the coast began to show signs of recovery. Native plants quickly re-established themselves. We enjoyed

Native coastal purple asters

Seaside Solution: Salt Spray on Windows

A constant annoyance of living by the sea is salt spray on windows. The crusty, thin, opaque film of salt interferes with our enjoyment of the view, particularly over the fall and winter months. A quick, easy, and effective way to clean salt deposits from glass is to use regular household ammonia: one part ammonia to five parts water. It is biodegradable, and at this strength it is not harmful to plants or animals.

- Simply dip a Swiffer fitted with liquid-holding fabric into the solution.
- Apply the solution to the glass starting at the top, just 1 cm (1/3 in.) from the windowpane to avoid drips.
- Then, using a squeegee, pull the liquid down from top to bottom.

Instant, squeaky clean glass. Enjoy the view!

Best way to clean salt spray off ocean-facing windows

the most beautiful purple asters in the fall of 2004, and these days, you wouldn't know that such a violent storm had hit our shores.

COASTAL WINTER CLIMATE

Lobster season resumes at the end of November, with colourful buoys once again bobbing up and down in our coves. When the fishers haul their traps up for the winter, usually mid-January, you know they've had it with the weather. This is the most erratic time of year at the coast. We get snow squalls, freezing rain, cold hard rain, mild sunny days, thaw, freeze, and thaw again. It is up and down. But snow doesn't "fall" here, it flies horizontally more often than vertically. Lack of good snow cover, sudden freeze and thaw episodes, and freezing rain can threaten the hardiest of plants. Covering roots over winter is a good idea the first year, but where I live, any cover gets blown away in no time, even when weighed down with rocks. On my windswept property, burlap tents act as a kite in strong wind. They don't last. This is, to me, too much futile work. So my plants have to be healthy and strong from the start.

Not all plants can tolerate seaside winter climate conditions (see chapter 3). Plants intended for the

Freezing rain on coastal plants

coastal environment not only need to be chosen well, they need to be ***planted*** well to increase their chances of survival. The greatest cause of plant failure at the coast is winter frost heave and that nasty, salty freezing rain that leaves a thick layer of ice on branches, encasing the newly set buds from the previous summer. Strong winds bend branches, causing the ice to snap off along with little buds. Plants that can tolerate severe pruning are the survivors of this kind of damage.

Another coastal winter issue is frost heave. The ground can freeze and thaw then freeze again several times a day! This erratic fluctuation in temperature is, by far, is the most detrimental to garden plants. Until they've had a couple of years to build a strong root system to anchor themselves, garden plants are prone to nearly completely popping out of the ground. A few simple steps at planting time can reduce the chances of this from happening:

- When planting in the spring (never in fall), make sure that surrounding soil is well loosened in order to make outward and downward root growth easier.
- Prepare a hole that is at least twice the size of the plant's root ball. Water well and press soil down firmly.
- When placing your new plant in the ground, ensure that there is a good-sized concave depression, about 5 cm (2 in.), from the surrounding soil surface. This will allow some up-and-down movement without the chance of the root ball rising above ground level.
- Fill the dip with mulch, peat moss, or rain-rinsed seaweed.

A nautical ornament breaks the monotony of a long winter by the sea.

Garden centres are always well stocked in attractive spring bloomers at the start of the growing season; it is difficult to resist buying a gorgeous rhododendron in bloom. Although I hadn't had good luck growing them before by the sea, this particular one, called Blue Baron, really caught my eye. The fact that it was labelled zone 4 and its leaves were slightly smaller than zone 5 cultivars seemed to make it a reasonable choice worth trying out. I

Coastal Tip

Where the snow accumulates, less wind; where no snow accumulates, too much wind.

This tree, killed by wind and salt spray, gets a Charlie Brown Christmas

thought it stood a good chance if planted in a well-protected spot, so I caved in and bought it. A part of our house has an indent, which gave the plant a wall on three sides. This appeared to be a very promising area to have a rhodo. We enjoyed its spring show immensely. And, because rhododendron is an evergreen, it was a pleasant sight to see greenery in the dead of winter.

During a sunny stroll though the yard one fine January afternoon, I discovered that my prized specimen was gone! My first thought was theft, but the soil had not been disturbed and the root ball was intact. I later retrieved the sad, rootless shrub from the shore. I remembered that there had been a brutal windstorm a few days before. Eventually, I discovered that the wind had caused the plant to oscillate so much that the stem had snapped off at the base. I don't think covering it up would have made any difference. It turned out that I had picked a very bad spot to plant something. I had not noticed until then that there was never any snow accumulation in that particular spot, which is very significant. Hurricanes and winter sea storms can spell disaster for garden plants. The only thing growing in that space now is a big piece of

Fresh new candlesticks on spring mugo pine

driftwood found after a storm, which I placed there as a memorial to my lost rhodo.

As emphasized in chapter 3, plants destined for a coastal garden should be hardy to (at least) two zones lower than prescribed for your general region. These cultivars will stand a much better chance of making it at the coast. Azalea is a better choice over rhododendron: it has smaller leaves that are less likely to act as little kites in the wind. Azalea "Popsicle" and Azalea "Northern Lights," both zone 4, are aptly named for their ability to withstand fierce winters.

Windburn on conifers is nothing to be alarmed about. In the case of mugo pine, it will be fine as long as you can still see new candles forming at the tip of branches. The same can be said for other shrubs and trees. As long as buds remain following a storm, they will come through just fine. The first couple of years are the most difficult on new plants at the coast.

Perseverance, as with patience, is a virtue at the coast for both gardeners and the plants we love. Four seasons by the sea has its challenges. Winter seems so long here, but on the upside, it affords us a good long rest from garden chores. We can retreat indoors, surround ourselves with seed and perennial catalogues, and imagine a new beginning.

ABOUT COASTAL CLIMATE CHANGE

Croucher Island stands about midway into St. Margarets Bay, Nova Scotia. There used to be a lighthouse there, where Maggie Boutilier and her family lived as lightkeepers from 1922 to 1944. In *Life on Croucher's Island*, her chronicle of their lives during that period, Maggie Boutilier writes, "The ice was so thick, the sea would crack it...the creaking and groaning at night was so severe a body could hardly sleep." The quote, written not so long ago, is about life on an island I can see from my window. Several passages refer to sea ice so thick that one could walk safely to the mainland to get provisions. Talk of riding horses and cars to nearby islands can still be heard in these parts—a thing of the past. It appears that signs of warming winters are increasing.

Even in my short time here in the bay (about twenty-five years), I have noticed climactic changes. During the months of January, February, and March, ice sheets used to form from the headwaters of the bay to the reaches of Croucher Island. Ice-fishing shacks in tranquil coves were a reliable sight during those months. These are no more. Some lobster fishers are able to leave their traps in the water all winter. Just a decade ago, this would have been impossible.

There is consensus among climatologists that atmospheric warming is indeed taking place. Much attention is given to which places will feel the greatest impact. In Canada, coastal areas and arctic climates will experience the most pronounced effects of global warming. Aboriginal people of the North have already seen dramatic changes in their own lifetimes. In the Arctic, elders have observed thinner sea ice and earlier snow melts. Caribou herds have diminished. There are sightings of malnourished polar bears, which depend on thick ice to hunt seal. Unfamiliar plant and insect species have migrated North. A colleague of mine who teaches about a hundred kilometers (sixty-two miles) north of Yellowknife told me of her fourth-graders coming across a ladybug in the schoolyard. They were terrified of it, thinking that it might be poisonous, so they killed it before it killed them and their teacher!

Locally, the Ecology Action Centre has published a fact sheet for the Maritimes that can be found online at ecologyaction.ca. Here are some important predictions for our coast. Some are quite alarming and, I am sure, controversial.

- Average global temperatures for the Maritimes are expected to rise between 1 and 3.5 degrees Celsius before the end of the century.

Land is lost to the sea

- Melting glaciers are expected to raise the sea level by 40–70 cm (1–2 ft.) over the next one hundred years.
- Coastal storm intensity and frequency will accelerate.
- Nova Scotia in particular is experiencing a gradual subsidence of its landmass by 1 cm (1/3 in.) yearly. This will exacerbate rising sea levels.
- Erosion and storm surge floods will present as more extreme events.
- The growing season is extending, but with potentially more plant pests and diseases, mostly in inland areas.

Maritime shorelines are certainly showing signs of advancing erosion. The little cove where I like to swim borders a coastal forest. A large tree stump, which is 1/2 m (1 1/2 ft.) underwater at low tide, is exposed for a while following a storm. This is evidence that the sea has claimed what was once the floor of an old-growth coastal forest. The first survey of this area was in 1918. It shows a 4 m- (13 ft.) wide road that followed the shore. That access is now well into the ordinary high-water mark. This is a remarkable change in one century, one lifetime. What more will I see of shifting shorelines if I live to be one hundred? Fortunately, these changes are gradual enough that we can adjust, prepare, and hopefully plan ahead.

Those of us who have lived along the shore for a while realize that these dynamic places are forever changing. The geology at water's edge is constantly responding to the warming coastal climate. It redefines itself after every blow and then stabilizes itself

Yucca or Adam's needle, a native of the Southwest United States, is a plant formally unknown to Atlantic coastal gardeners. It is a recent introduction to our increasingly mild coastal winters.

An old fishing boat called "My Chance" that was damaged in a storm gets a second chance at life in this coastal garden.

Naturalized garden phlox among the coastal grasses are able to withstand the coastal elements.

once again. Historically, Maritimers have put a lot of energy and resources into intercepting the ocean's urge to expand, but natural ecosystems are so much better at absorbing the impact of coastal storms than any of our interventions. Wetlands and native coastal plants act as a buffer against ensuing coastal climate change, and can soften its impact.

Coastal plants are a good natural guard against erosion.

As stated at the outset, the seaside climate can indeed be frightful at times. Garden plants, once established, are very forgiving. Coddle and pamper them only in their first year. After that, let them struggle through what the sea throws at them. Dry spells, for example, force roots down deeper in search of moisture, while frequent watering leads to shallow, weak roots. Struggling plants will build a stronger grip around rocks and become better able to endure the worst of seaside conditions. Gardening at the coast is a bit of a battle, but don't give up the ship so easily. Hardship, it is said, builds character.

7

SEASIDE SOIL SOS

In the spring, at the end of the day, you should smell like dirt.
—Margaret Atwood—

We would all agree that life as we know it could not exist without air and water, but few of us would think to give soil the same recognition. Soil is the beginning of the terrestrial food chain. It supports the micro life forms needed to support more complex life forms up to and including humans. People cannot do without soil any more than they can do without air and water. The modernization of soil cultivation techniques has led to concerns as grave as overfishing and water and air pollution. Soil is as precious and as finite a resource as water. I think that hands-on seaside gardeners understand this best because many of us feel deprived of good-quality soil and have to work hard at keeping it fertile with composting and regular amendments (more on this later).

Serious gardeners have a relationship with their soil. We feel it to gauge its texture, moisture, and warmth. We feed it by composting. We cajole it by turning it over. We take measures to prevent erosion. We also defend soil by mulching and keeping aggressive plants out. Soil, dirt, ground, earth—whatever people call it—is where gardening begins.

Native plants are able to grow in a variety of soils that would leave garden plants lacking essential nutrients. Soil specialists can determine whether or not your ground is suitable for gardening simply by looking at its colour and texture. Certain soil types need more amendments than others and some types are

Many coastal gardeners resort to imported soil.

hopeless. Generally speaking, darker soils (deep reds, browns, blacks) are best for gardening because they are highest in organic matter and therefore require the least amount of amendments, provided there is good depth. Trees need at least 1 m (3 ft.), shrubs and root vegetables need 1/2 m, and so on, to lawn, which needs only about 5–6 cm (2 in.) of "good" soil depth. Conversely, the most troublesome soils are lighter in colour. Reddish-pink soils are predominantly clay. Orange/yellow soils indicate high iron. These are both hardpan materials that lead to poor drainage. Tan- and grey-coloured soils are usually sandy or silty in nature, and as a result quickly leach out essential nutrients.

The health of your coastal plants will depend largely on the depth and quality of the soil that houses their roots. Anything you want to plant, with the exception of native coastal species of course, will require getting the soil ready. By this, I mean improving soil depth and fertility. After that, it is simply a matter of basic maintenance and replenishing of nutrients before and after each growing season—that is, if you have soil to begin with! Most soils can be corrected to improve fertility, but along the northern Atlantic coast it is often too shallow, acidic, and rocky. That was the case for our newly constructed oceanfront home in Indian Harbour, Nova Scotia: the lot consisted of nothing but black spruce. It would have taken us several decades of composting to achieve a workable quantity of optimal soil for gardening there. So for that reason, we felt it necessary to import a couple of truckloads of good farm soil to get started.

A GOOD FOUNDATION

Gardening is dynamic. Much like cooking, it is not an exact science, but akin to following the Canada's Food Guide for eating well. As with our own dietary requirements, there are a few basic criteria to follow in order to achieve a balanced "garden-soil diet." Gardening is not so much a matter of nourishing plants, but rather a matter of nourishing the soil in which they grow. The best start we can give our coastal gardens is a good foundation: fertile soil.

What is fertile soil? That is a question that I am not qualified to answer. But I would like, in this chapter, to offer my layperson's abbreviated explanation, based on my experience with coastal gardening and a university course on the nature of soil.

Entire books have been written on the topic of soil composition. Be forewarned, though, that most of these texts treat the matter of soil quality in biochemical terms. For those of you with a strong background in the sciences, especially biochemistry, do go to a source that treats the subject of soil in depth. Such resources are available through most public libraries. Here are a few recent titles that may be of interest: *Teaming with Microbes: The Organic Gardener's Guide to the Soil Food Web* by Jeff Lowenfels, *The Nature and Properties of Soils* by Nyle C. Brady and Ray R. Weil, and *Life in the Soil: A Guide for Naturalists and Gardeners* by James B. Nardi.

The study of the nature of soil is multidimensional. Surface, depth, and geological time are all intricately involved. I asked soil scientist Dr. Phil Warman, a former professor at the Nova Scotia Agricultural College and McGill University, for a short spiel on the nature of seaside soils in our North Atlantic coastal climate. Professor Warman says that our seaside soils are generally low in pH and fertility, with phosphorous especially lacking. As a consequence, coastal soils are low in biological activity. "The gardener has to amend soil regularly with good-quality compost, manure or completely balanced fertilizers," says Warman. He insists on gardeners getting their soil tested in order to know exactly what is lacking and, consequently, what is needed to bring it up to peak performance. He also added, "An equal content of N-P-K [those three numbers on all-purpose fertilizers] is considered balanced by many, but it is not appropriate for our seaside garden soils, since we are low in phosphorous, and lacking essential micronutrients plus calcium and magnesium."

Do not underestimate the nature of soil. I was surprised to learn that there are more micro-organisms in one spoonful of fertile soil than there are people on earth. What an astonishing thought! This microbial activity is essential to plant health. Soil organisms are responsible for breaking down essential elements into forms that plants can use. Good soil fertility is essentially a workable—preferably crumb-like—soil structure, with high microbial activity. These organisms are most numerous and productive in soils with a pH of 6.5. Levels from 6 to 5.5 leave the soil too acidic for micro-organisms to thrive. Soils with a pH of 7 or higher are just as inhospitable to biological activity (note that alkaline soils are not an issue at the coast). Another important factor in maintaining soil fertility is to ensure that your chosen gardening spot has good drainage, or the essential micro-organisms will "drown," allowing room for other offensive smelling organisms to set up camp.

What causes pH levels to be so low in many coastal soils? Well, if you live by the sea, airborne salt is inevitable. And salt is an acid. Wind and fog are constant events that can last for several days. Salt accumulates and is easily saturated into the ground. I thought the title of this chapter, "Seaside Soil SOS," would be fitting because this Morse code message means distress at sea. Coastal soils are too high in salt, leading to poor fertility. Salt contributes to high soil acidity, limiting gardening possibilities. Although a naturally occurring substance and an essential part of the chemistry in most living organisms, as humans, we know

Coastal Tips for Importing Soil

Dark soils are an indication of high organic material content and fertiliy.

The following are a few common terms used for imported soil:

- "Fill," more often called "clean fill," is earth-based uncontaminated material used to infill a depression, a steep bank, or hole in order to level the ground. It can be anything from rock, bricks, or concrete fragments to sand and gravel, or a combination of either. This material can serve as a useful base for drainage but is not a suitable growing medium for gardens.
- "Topsoil" is a soil of average quality acceptable for lawns when applied at least 5 cm (2 in.) deep. It is not sufficiently rich in nutrients and fertility to support gardening.
- "Garden soil," preferably organic, is what you should import for your seaside gardening needs. This is a prepared soil with a good balance of humus, clay, silt, sand, and other organic materials rich in biological activity.

Coastal Tip

Granular lime is best as it is heavy and drops to the ground immediately, whereas the powdered form, although faster acting, gets swept off to sea where it is neither helpful nor healthful to aquatic life. A few good, hard rains quickly dissolve pelleted lime and push its particles into the soil, the incorporation of which is always beneficial for speeding up the process of neutralizing sodium.

that an overconsumption of salt leads to short- and long-term health issues. The same applies to essential soil organisms and, subsequently, garden plants.

The easiest antidote to high salt content in soil is lime application (the calcium and magnesium Professor Warman spoke about earlier). Apply lime generously twice each year—in early spring and again in the fall—to ensure time for effective salt neutralization, thereby raising your soil pH before planting time. Many inland gardeners only lime once every two or three years, but the coastal gardener must not procrastinate.

SUPERIOR COASTAL COMPOST

During my pursuit of successful seaside gardens for this book, I stumbled upon an amazing find, hidden right in my own community of Indian Harbour. I discovered an entire garden of plants with coastal characteristics. In chapter 2 I introduce you to the architect of this masterpiece: Walter Ostrum, ceramics artist and retired teacher from the Nova Scotia College of Art and Design University. When Walter purchased this (one-hectare) seaside property in the 1970s, it was a barren, rocky, windswept field. Today it is a flourishing garden of mature trees, shrubs, ground covers, and a multitude of flowering plants.

When Walter arrived on the property he understood well the challenge of improving his land's poor, shallow soil. He worked with nature rather than attempting to alter her: no soil was imported; no commercial fertilizers were used. To get started, Walter began with harvesting as much seaweed as he could gather from his shore. It was piled in high heaps to get rinsed by the rain and decompose. Enormous quantities of this nutrient-rich "dark slop" were folded into the original soil along with bags of leaves that he had gathered from curbs in Halifax. This was an ongoing practice on his property. With time, interesting native plants began to move in. Walter noticed which plants were thriving and added only similar cultivars. No special care was necessary since these plants were

Walter Ostrum's property in the 1970s

Walter Ostrum's property in 2013

bred from specimens whose origin resembled that of his coastal conditions (for more, see pp. 27 and 200). The success of all the plants growing here bear witness to the importance of starting with deep, nutrient-rich soil. Gardening from seaweed-based compost is nothing short of a miracle.

Keeping the soil fertile is imperative. You wouldn't go a year without being fed, and neither can soil. This is especially important to remember by the sea, where plants experience more stress than usual. All plantings take up nutrients that must be replenished in order to remain healthy and hardy. Chemical fertilizers are not a remedy for depleted, shallow, acidic soil. While occasional feedings can enhance plant performance—giving them stronger stems, roots, and flowers—they do nothing to improve soil texture, structure, and depth. A generous serving of homemade plant-based compost is the best way to improve soil quality and to replenish what has been lost—and more.

I am a convert of seaweed-based compost as a superior, natural soil conditioner. (See chapter 8 for more details.) In its various forms—wet, dry, or as tea—seaweed serves specific functions. For coastal gardeners, seaweed is the best soil enhancement material available. First of all, it is free. Second, it is natural. And third, it is bountiful along most northern coastlines.

In all of my research on using seaweed for improving soil, I have encountered nothing but accolades.

Landed seaweed ready for harvest

Late fall the compost heap is turned over onto garden soil and left to rest, free-standing, all winter.

Suffice it to say, pioneers knew much more than they understood; they discovered that seaweed improved soil fertility without knowing quite why. Even today, it is still not fully understood why seaweed is proven to increase crop nutrition and yield. There may be a good reason for which more research has not been done. For starters, most of the world's agriculture takes place inland. If seaweed were used, it would have to be purchased. Secondly, seaweed needs to be processed for commercial use, so that it is efficient to transport and easy to spread. From an economical standpoint, seaweed is a pricey natural fertilizer for inland gardeners. Seaside gardeners, on the other hand, have easy access to it in its raw, pure form. We are sitting on gold!

My plant-based compost pile is a combination of kitchen scraps, yard waste, and, of course, rain-rinsed seaweed. I am careful to layer these three materials with a bit of garden soil in between to introduce the soil organisms that will speed up the process of breaking it all down into a rich, black, sweet-smelling compost. Keeping a plant-based compost pile throughout the year is a basic gardening practice with many benefits. It diverts essential nutrients from landfills and/or distant industrial composting establishments. The home compost is your direct supply of essential micro- and macronutrients to be returned to the soil. Composted seaweed is cited over and over as being a perfect balance of all three essential elements: Nitrogen, Phosphorus, and Potassium (N-P-K), which include other essential trace elements.

It is a spring ritual to incorporate some of this rich decomposed organic matter into our seaside garden beds. Food crops are the most needy. Having the compost pile close to the produce garden makes for easy transfer. Come spring, we till it in deeply, especially for root crops. Allow a couple of weeks (longer if cold weather persists) for biological activity to resume before planting the vegetable garden.

Although it's a complex biological process, achieving good quality home compost is quite elementary. There are two key points to consider: pile it up and provide aeration. Quantity provides the micro- and macro-organisms (bugs and earthworms) with shelter from the elements, offering them the warmth and time to do their job undisturbed. Piling up plant-based materials is easy. Providing aeration, on the other hand, can be a lot of work. Turning the pile over often is recommended, but is way too labour intensive for me, so I've shared my "lazy composter's technique" with you (right).

Like humans, the micro-organisms responsible for breaking down plant-based material into rich compost need air to thrive. Fresh grass clippings and wet seaweed are excellent sources of nitrogen, but when piled up high they are notorious for smothering essential little life forms. Some gardeners spread it out to dry before throwing it on the compost pile. When dried, the weight and volume of seaweed and grass clippings shrink by more than half, making transfer much easier. This is a great compost solution if you have plenty of space for spreading. If not, fresh grass clippings and wet seaweed are best composted in layers of no more than 30 cm (1 ft.) thick between layers of kitchen scraps and yard waste.

Because these materials are not always conveniently available in just the right quantity at the right time, depending on the time of year I end up with what seems like a truckload of one or the other all at once. Nevertheless, I pile it all on, but with a little trick to ensure air flow. Before I reveal *how* I do it, here is why: I like to keep composting as cost-effective, simple, and labour-free as possible, so I do not use a commercial composter. Some gardeners invest in fancy composting units. These are mostly used to keep the composting cycle tidy. Some units pivot to turn the material over. These are by no means necessary. Here is what works well for me and gives great results.

THE EFFICIENT "LAZY" COMPOSTER'S TECHNIQUE

To compensate for not turning the compost pile over regularly, I have found other ways to keep it aerated. For starters, I do not keep the pile contained, but at the back of the vegetable garden. Where the garden ends, composting begins. In other words, the compost heap is free-standing: there are no walls, so air is all around. That is the first "lazy" step.

The interior of the pile is where micro-organisms suffer most from lack of oxygen. To help prevent this, I pile up large quantities of wet seaweed or fresh grass clippings and criss-cross branchy twigs (saved from last year's pruning of trees and shrubs) about every

Criss-crossed sticks provide air pockets as plant-based materials decompose into compost

Twigs saved for keeping the compost pile aerated

Old spruce boughs, quills off, are an excellent aerator for the compost pile.

30 cm (1 ft.) of material, then add another layer of plant material. This very simple tactic provides plenty of little air pockets for the pile to "breathe." Place a row of twigs in one direction and another row in the other direction. Old spruce boughs from the forest floor work just as well, if not better! Save your old Christmas tree.

You will know that microbes are hard at work when the height of the compost material shrinks quickly and is warm to the touch, even on cold days. Late fall, when it is time to put the vegetable garden to rest, is the only time I turn the pile over. To do so, I toss the compost over from top to bottom onto the garden soil in front of it, again in a free-standing heap. It will rest there over the winter months and continue to decompose while I start a fresh new pile in the same spot for the following year. Come early spring, I spread the ripe, old pile over the garden soil and till the material in. That's it. As a fellow gardener once said: "Compost happens."

I am often asked if undesirable "weeds" can be added on the compost pile. Absolutely! The root balls of weeds are packed with active micro-organisms, but if pulled and added to the pile while full of seed, you risk reintroducing undesirable plants back into your garden the following year. So it is wise to discard seedy plants away from the garden and compost pile. Seeds are killed only when the compost pile reaches a high temperature of at least 50 degrees Celsius (120 degrees Fahrenheit). The larger the pile, the hotter it gets and the faster it decomposes. Layering fresh grass clippings or wet seaweed is a great way to give the compost pile a "hot flash."

As mentioned earlier, decomposed plant-based material not only adds nutrients to average and poor soils, it improves soil structure and texture. What about animal waste? Yes, this is also true of manure, but it cannot be from just any animal. Never use human or carnivorous animal manures for home composting, as they are high-risk carriers of dangerous-to-humans organisms. Decomposed herbivore/ruminant manures are basically plant-based composts, but there are a number of drawbacks to using the dung of chicken, horses, sheep, and cows, particularly in the vegetable garden.

Unless you have access to a farm, manure has to be bought. Incurring such a cost defeats a central purpose of growing your own food: saving dollars! Seaweed, yard waste, and table scraps are free, and, in turn, divert otherwise nutrient-rich materials from your local landfill. Obtaining manure directly from a farm may be free but it likely contains undigested seed, which will add exponentially to the chore of weeding. The case could also be made that livestock waste often contains medical residue from treatments against parasites, from antibiotics, growth hormones, etc., which can be absorbed by the plants that end up on your plate.

While animal waste is high in biological activity, it contains potentially harmful pathogens, even when "well rotted." I especially avoid applying manure to my vegetable garden for this reason. There have been many recently reported cases of E. coli contamination on produce causing illness and even death. Commercial brands of garden manures are supposedly treated and free of seed and harmful bacteria but are pricey compared to making your own plant based compost—and I use a lot of it. Also, I don't like the thought of wallowing in animal excrement in sandals with my bare hands while tending the garden during those really warm summer days.

Have you heard the one about the dear elderly couple?

The wife stops and says, "Honey, what is that in the garden?"

"I'm not sure," says her dear ol' husband. He bends down closer. "That looks like poop," he says. He presses his thumb into the stuff and brings it up to his nose for a sniff. "Smells like poop...." He then, to his wife's horror, licks his thumb and says, "Tastes like poop, too. Yup, that's poop all right.... Good thing we didn't step in it."

BEAN-BASED HOME SOIL TEST

April is finally here. The ground has thawed but night frosts are still imminent. It is time to till last fall's compost pile into the vegetable garden soil, along with another good helping of lime. Then, I'll let the mixture sit until the end of the month. With longer, warmer days, biological activity in the soil increases, and in turn, so does soil fertility.

It is now time to test the soil to see if its pH balance and nutrient levels are suitable to begin planting. Most gardeners agree that taking soil samples to a lab every four or five years is a good idea. There are commercial soil-test gadgets available to home gardeners, but I don't find them as reliable as the plants themselves: optimal soil = healthy plants; soil that is lacking = stressed plants.

Seeds left over from last year are fine for the home soil test.

For peace of mind, I like to do several simple home soil tests between early March and April to see how my soil is doing. After all, this soil will be used throughout the property as needed for all other seaside flowering plants and shrubs. My simple soil test is not as accurate as a lab test, but it is still a good indicator of soil fertility.

Be sure to label your soil samples, or the test will be worthless.

Plant performance says it all. I have found snap beans work well for this test, as they require a soil pH of 6.5 (ideal for most crops), a balanced N-P-K, and they do well indoors (for a time, as long as they have a south-facing window and are watered frequently). The healthy plants get transplanted to the garden.

Soil sample from raised beds is obviously doing poorly when compared to samples from other parts of the garden.

The first step to testing your garden soil is to take samples from various parts of the gardening area. In my case, four samples suffice. I place the soil in 6 cm- (2 1/2 in.-) wide pots, clearly labelled with the area of sample taken, and then bring them indoors for about ten days to allow micro-organisms time to warm up and get active. I then plant three snap bean seeds (left over from last year) in each pot to ensure seed viability and thin them down to one—the strongest. It is evident within just a few days which parts of the garden are either too low in pH or lacking a major nutrient or two. This particular year, it was apparent from my initial soil test that something was lacking in the soil from my raised beds. Sprouting was slower and growth was delayed compared to my other soil samples.

It can be difficult to figure out what may be lacking when a plant shows signs of stress in a particular soil sample: slow germination, tiny or shrivelled leaves, yellowing, stunted growth. At the coast, the first suspicion should be low pH. But if you are a serious composter who faithfully incorporates lime in your soil, there is likely something else going on. To rule out low pH as the cause for struggling bean sprouts, do another test using extra lime. Here's how I do it:

- Dissolve 1 teaspoon lime in 1 cup rainwater, then pour 5 ml. (1 tsp.) of the solution in about 500 ml. (2 cups) garden soil from the area of the garden in question. Mix well. (Diluted molasses (1:5) in a

Coastal Tip

Bean plants started indoors will likely begin to flower before they are ready to be planted outside. There is no need to worry if you don't have available pollinators—beans produce self-pollinating flowers! Bees are not necessary. Pollination occurs before the flower opens, since the anthers (male pollen-producing part of the flower) are pushed up against the stamen (sticky female pollen receiver). Plant them out after all danger of frost has passed in a setting out of reach to deer. Enjoy the unusually early harvest.

Self-pollinating bean flowers

Earlier harvest than seeds started outside

soil sample is another way to raise pH and excite micro-organisms. You may replace the lime solution with diluted molasses.)

- Put the new soil sample in a plant pot.
- Keep the sample in the house for a couple of weeks to allow biochemical reactions to take place before planting the bean seeds.
- Plant three or four seeds in the soil sample.
- Provide warmth and light (a south-facing window sill).

If the young plants now thrive, you can conclude that the pH needed to be higher in that area of the garden. If they still show signs of stress, it is time to take that soil sample to a lab for testing.

Even with extra lime in my second soil test, the bean sprouts struggled. Something else was lacking in my raised beds' soil. I then noticed that there were no earthworms in the raised beds whereas the main garden had some in just about every shovelful. I inferred that perhaps the soil from my second test lacked beneficial organisms, which had limited access to this area of the garden (the raised beds are lined with old reclaimed bricks as walkways). Also, nutrients tend to leach out more easily in raised beds than in the main garden. Earthworms are always a welcome addition. Whenever I see one, I throw it in one of the raised beds. For an extra measure of care, I also gave the soil in the raised beds a dose of seaweed tea (see p. 111). A few weeks later, I repeated the "bean test" from the raised-beds' soil alongside samples from the main garden. They were compatible. Soil issue solved!

8

The Versatility of Seaweed

Call us not weeds—we are flowers of the sea.
—E. L. Aveline—

The sea is certainly a different world than the one we know on land, but there is one important similarity: both have plants. Aquatic plants, too, need light and survive by photosynthesis. From kelp forests several metres high to low, rock-clinging, moss-like plants, the ocean is fertile ground for vegetation. There are seasons here as well. Now and then, the sea floor sheds her leathery mat, what we call seaweed. It floats ashore in abundant quantities. Gathering sea plants is a time-tested tradition in the Maritimes. I would be remiss not to mention the virtues of aquatic plants in this book.

Seaweed can play an important role in the health of seaside soils and the plants we grow. Sea plants are harvested for various purposes. Prince Edward Island enjoys a strong export of Irish moss—an aptly named little plant used as a natural thickener in food and pharmaceuticals. Dulse is harvested commercially in

Seaweed, a lobster's habitat for shelter and foraging

both New Brunswick and Nova Scotia as a versatile culinary delicacy and health food. And to the seaside gardener, composted seaweed is "liquid gold."

SEAWEED FOR THE GARDEN: METHODS OF APPLICATION

Regarded by some as "sea waste," landed seaweed is to the gardener a free, organic fertilizer guaranteed to increase soil fertility. It breaks down into a balanced formula of all the essential ingredients for plant health: nitrogen (leaf growth), phosphorous (flowers, fruit, and root formation), potassium (stem health and hardiness), and more! An impressive study was recently conducted at the Nova Scotia Agricultural College that supports seaweed as a superior fertilizer (search "fertilizer from the sea" online, or visit innovationcanada.ca).

The advantages of fertilizing the garden with seaweed as opposed to chemical fertilizers are many: improved soil structure by humus formation, increased aeration, moisture retention, and the encouragement in the growth of a wealth of beneficial micro-organisms. Unlike manure, seaweed is safe for handling at all stages, from fresh to decomposed. Furthermore, since seaweed releases nutrients naturally and gradually, there is no danger of creating an N-P-K imbalance or overdose, as can be the case with the use of chemical fertilizers.

As highlighted in chapter 9 (p. 127), slugs loathe seaweed! It serves at once to keep slugs out and nourish the soil as it breaks down! Should you have issues with cats using the garden as their litter box, surround the area with dried crunchy seaweed. A cat will avoid stepping on it, and will turn around rather than leap into the garden. When the seaweed gets wet, you

Kelpful Hint

Gardeners should know that there are regulations around the collection of any natural materials on Nova Scotia shores. Collecting a bucketful periodically from your own oceanfront is not a matter of concern. For greater quantities, the Department of Natural Resources does issue permits, at no cost, for harvesting up to 7 1/2 m² (10 sq. yd.). Harvesting from provincial parks is not permitted.

A bucketful of seaweed here and there poses no threat to the environment.

will be entertained by the cat repeatedly testing it with one paw, like a hot soup, then deciding to go elsewhere to do her "business."

Landed seaweed is so common that there should be no need to scrape it off the rocks live. That could cause an imbalance in the marine ecosystem. Many creatures depend on it for shelter from predators, for laying their eggs, for larvae stages, and for places to find food. Sea plants, as with terrestrial plants, go through life stages. They too perish and then are washed ashore naturally. Before using seaweed in the garden, it is important to have it free of sea water.

Rain-rinsed seaweed can serve many purposes for gardeners.

Garden plants do not need salt. Significant amounts of salt in the soil contribute to soil acidity, can prohibit growth and lead to dieback. The best time to collect seaweed is following a good hard rain (or pile it up somewhere until it rains). There are several methods for applying seaweed to the garden: wet, dry, in the compost pile, and as "tea" (p. 111).

Wet Mulch

This can be any type of fresh (wet) seaweed. It can be applied directly under and around plants but it is not considered "decorative" mulch since the colour is rather mixed and predominantly rust in hue, but does darken eventually. This is utilitarian mulch, used between the rows of the vegetable garden or under perennials for winter protection. It keeps weeds down when sufficiently deep (10–15 cm [4–6 in.]) and fertilizes the soil as it breaks down. Seaweed application between plants, wet or dry, also serves as a slug deterrent (more on p. 127).

Dry Mulch

Instead of using pricey store-bought black mulch, look for black dried rockweed at the shore to place under your plants. A common species of seaweed called knotted wrack eventually turns black when it lands in clumps above the regular high-water mark. After undergoing several wet–dry cycles between rainy and sunny days, it almost looks like "cow patties" (p. 110) but airy and brittle once dry. The crisp clumps or "patties" can be used as is for mulching or crushed.

Rain-rinsed seaweed between plants introduces nutrients to soil as it breaks down, and acts as a weed-suppressing mulch as well as a slug deterrent.

To crumble the clumps, simply place them in a large bag, like a large dog food bag, or on an old bed sheet folded over. Stomp over it repeatedly until desired crumb size is achieved then spread it where needed. Some gardeners like to shred dry seaweed using the lawnmower. It is then raked up. Either way, the result is a beautiful black material that makes foliage and blooms stand out dramatically.

This "dry mulch" eventually breaks down into a rich plant food mid- season, so a second application is required to keep weeds down and freshen up the black backdrop.

Simply apply to the base of plants or as you would regular garden mulch

The Compost Pile

Wet or dry seaweed is piled up to decompose. The larger the pile, the faster is breaks down. It turns to a molasses-like liquid from the bottom up quite quickly in warm weather (two weeks, more or less). So place the pile where you would like the nutrient-rich fluids to seep into the ground. Seaweed can also be added to your existing compost pile, where it seems to

Dry mulch at the base of seaside lavender

disappear in no time. But its nutrients are definitely present, playing an important role in improving soil structure and creating a wealth of biological activity that contributes to plant growth and health. (See "Superior Coastal Compost," p. 96, for more.)

SEAWEED FOR THE KITCHEN: THE NUTRITIONAL VALUE OF DULSE

Here in the Maritimes, the seasoning of the sea is an aquatic plant called dulse. More than that, this sea vegetable is regarded as a natural health food with exceptional nutritional value. I am fortunate to have had access to dulse from a young age. It is said to be an acquired taste. Those of us who like it, like it a lot. We enjoy it as a healthy and wholesome Maritime snack or as a versatile ingredient in cooking. Ample information is available online about the wealth of vitamin and mineral content of dulse.

Jody Braveman, a health professional and writer in Seattle wrote an article called *The Benefits of Dulse Seaweed:* www.livestrong.com/article/418798-the-benefits-of-dulse-seaweed, in which she describes dulse as a super food. According to her sources at Eden Foods, dulse contains trace amounts of every dietary mineral needed by humans and is a rich source of vitamins A, C, and E, and B vitamins, including calcium, potassium, magnesium, iron, zinc, and iodide. It also contains essential enzymes that produce energy from sugars during digestion. Braveman recommends supplementing our diets with dulse as a whole food instead of using synthetic supplements.

Sea vegetables are plants also high in protein—a great alternative for those who do not consume animal products. Braveman declares that, weight for weight, sea plants are more easily digested and contain more minerals and vitamins than land plants. For those on a calorie-restrictive diet, dulse is also lower in fat and calories than other protein sources.

As an example of the superior nutritional value of natural dulse as a snack, I decided to compare it with Lay's Simply Natural Sea Salt Flavored Thick Cut Potato Chips (facing page).

Looking to the nutritional labels of both dulse and the chips, the difference was remarkable. An equal amount of dulse is a fraction of the calories: 20 compared with 270. The sodium intake for dulse is less than half that of these potato chips and with a much reduced amount of carbohydrates.

The protein percentile for potato chips may appear higher than that of dulse but in grams, it is actually more than six times denser in mass than dulse. Therefore, dulse is much higher, by mass, in protein than potato chips. That also explains the differences in vitamin C. Dulse is certainly superior in calcium and iron content.

HARVESTING DULSE

Harvesting dulse, or "dulsing," has long been a bit of a mystery to me even as a Maritimer. It grows in very specific types of coastlines. New Brunswick—in particular Grand Manan Island—harvests it commercially. Here in Nova Scotia, we enjoy a moderate harvest, found in abundance at the headwaters

Dried knotted wrack looks like a cow patty.

KELPFUL HINT: SEAWEED TEA

Wet or dry seaweed put in a large bucket and topped with fresh water will result in a condensed concentration of black "seaweed tea" in as soon as two weeks, when left to stew in a hot sunny location. The longer it is left, the denser the liquid becomes. The darker the liquid, the more concentrated the nutrients. When it becomes as dark as a black coffee, most gardeners recommend diluting it to one part "seaweed tea," two parts fresh water.

Feed seaweed tea to the base of plants. Where plants are small and dense, tea may get on leaves and flowers, partially blocking out sunlight. In this case, sprinkle the plants with a bit of fresh water to wash off the dark liquid.

Pouring seaweed "tea" into a watering can to which fresh water will be added

of the Bay of Fundy. So, for the book, I turned to a long-time family friend who would know all about dulsing: Melba Shute. This lovely lady grew up along a coastline renowned for the highest tides in the world: near Parrsboro, Nova Scotia. Incidentally, this area also boasts the lowest tides in the world, where the sea floor is exposed for many, many metres out.

Melba took me dulsing down a beaten path to a little-known beach that she frequented as a child between Parrsboro and Advocate Harbour.

NUTRITIONAL FACTS Per 30 potato chips		NUTRITIONAL FACTS Per 1/3 cup dulse	
50 g (about 1/3 cup compacted)		(about 7 g compacted)	
Amount	**% Daily Value**	**Amount**	**% Daily Value**
Calories 270		Calories 20	
Fat 16 g	25%	Fat 0 g	0%
Saturated fat 1.5 g	9%	Saturated Fat 0 g	0%
Cholesterol 0 mg	0%	Cholesterol 0 mg	0%
Sodium 260 mg 1	1%	Sodium 120 mg	5%
Carbohydrate 27 g	9%	Carbohydrates 3 g	1%
Fiber 2 g	8%	Fiber 2 g	8%
Protein 4 g		Protein 2 g	
Vitamin A	0%	Vitamin A	0%
Vitamin C	20%	Vitamin C	2%
Calcium	0%	Calcium	2%
Iron	8%	Iron	15%

Melba collecting dulse

The scenery was stunning. I learned that timing is of essence for gaining access to fresh dulse growing off rocks. Ideally, dulsing is best done during the two lowest tides of the year. Locals in many areas call these "dulsing" tides. There is only a two- to three-day window for easy access to the savoury sea plant. You can check for precise dates on the most extreme low tides online: www.bayoffundytourism.com/tides/times.

As the tide went out, I was surprised to see patches of the sea floor densely covered in huge, long sheets of sea plants. This reddish-brown kelp was fresh, live dulse. A single leaf can reach over 1 m (3 ft.) in length, not counting the stem. It was taught that dulse is collected and put into mesh bags to allow excess sea water to drain, and then, traditionally, spread thinly over beach rocks well above the high-water mark, to dry naturally in sunny summer breezes.

Dulse should never be exposed to rain or it will rot. If rain threatens, dulse can be hung to dry in an outbuilding, like a watertight shed or garage. It can also be brought in the house if you don't mind that salty/fishy smell while it dehydrates. Depending on humidity, it can take from four hours to two days for dulse to cure. It is at its best when it still has a bit of moisture: dry to the touch but pliable. Once it reaches this stage, dulse turns a lovely dark hue of purple/maroon. It is now ready to enjoy as a versatile sea snack, herb, or vegetable throughout the year. Extras should be kept sealed in plastic or in a jar, with the sea salt acting as a preservative. Dulse has an extremely long shelf life when stored away from sunlight and fluctuations in humidity.

Low tide exposes live dulse

Dulse goes from brown to purple as it dries

WAYS TO ENJOY DULSE AS FOOD

It is said that enjoyment of dulse as a savoury snack or in a recipe is an acquired taste. The most common complaint is that it is too salty. This is simply due to the fact that it has been left coated in seawater to "cure." Sea salt is actually what preserves dulse from breaking down. Breads, buns, soups, salads, pasta or rice dishes, even potatoes and other vegetables all lend themselves well to its flavour. I have a friend who even puts it in her pizza dough and calls it "Acadian pizza"! Where recipes call for salt, use dulse. It not only meets the salt required of a dish, but adds valuable nutrients that regular table salt doesn't. Following are many ways to use dulse in the kitchen. For those new to this healthy sea plant, keep an open mind. Dulse is a very versatile, natural, and nutritious food.

Dulse as a quick snack can take many forms. It can certainly be eaten as is. If salt intake is a concern, there are ways of reducing salt content before consuming it. Much of the salt will come off dulse when rubbed between your fingers or with a dampened paper towel, just before consuming. It can also be soaked briefly in fresh water before eating, which gives it a bit of a crunch. But if soaked for more than ten minutes, dulse will begin to break down. A quick dip in fresh water will suffice. After being dipped to preferred consistency, dulse can also be left to air dry for a few hours. Be sure to consume rinsed dulse the same day.

Dulse chips or "sea chips" can be either microwaved or fried. To prepare, separate dulse leaves into single layers, or "sheets," as much as possible. Tear sheets into in chip-sized pieces and toss into a bit of canola oil in a non-stick frying pan. As soon as they turn green, the chips are ready. Pat them with paper towel and enjoy the crunchy, nutty chips as you would regular potato chips. An oil-free way to prepare sea chips is to microwave them just five to ten seconds (depending on microwave), until they are tan in colour. For low-salt dulse chips, rub some salt off before cooking.

Dulse is great as a savoury garnish over favourite dishes where salt might be required, or with

Dulse chips

Shredded dulse over garden salad greens and a dribble of olive oil

under-salted meals of pasta, rice, soups, meats, seafood, casseroles, potatoes and other vegetables, and in salads. Just a little addition will whet the appetite. Shredded dulse also adds visual interest and nutrients to food. Simply fold a handful of dulse and shred using scissors.

Dulse bread, buns, biscuits, and stuffing are just a few ways to be creative and adventurous with dulse in the kitchen. All that is required is to add it to your favourite recipe instead of regular salt. Put in three times the amount of crushed dulse to the amount of salt called for. Fifteen ml (3 tsp) crushed, flaked, or shredded dulse equal approximately 5 ml (1 tsp) salt, but with a subtle taste of the sea and extra nutrient goodness.

A dulse-filled salt shaker can replace regular table salt with the bonus of added nutrients and flavour from the sea. It only requires crushing brittle, dry dulse and pouring it into a salt shaker. It can be used this way on its own or in combination with other savoury herbs and spices, like ground peppercorns, coriander, paprika, parsley, and chives. Before crushing dulse, allow it to air-dry until brittle (about one day depending on humidity). Place it in an envelope then press and bend it in all directions or flatten it using a rolling pin. Use your

Use dulse instead of table salt. It also makes a great-looking garnish.

Experiment using crushed dulse with various favourite spices.

Dulse instead of salt in homemade breads is as flavourful and artful as it is healthful.

Dulse Spice Blend on whatever is going on the BBQ, even on your morning eggs or in a grilled cheese. The possibilities are endless. Be creative and adventurous. The following is a standard blend we enjoy.

DULSE SPICE BLEND

* 250 ml (1 cup) packed very dry dulse
* 60 ml (1/4 cup) dry coriander seed
* 15 ml (1 tbsp) dill seed
* 30 ml (2 tbsp) cracked flax seed
* 5 ml (1 tsp) mustard seed
* 30 ml (2 tbsp) cracked pepper

Place dulse and coriander seed on a good size sheet of wax paper. Fold in two and crush using a rolling pin or crush using a mortar and pestle. Mix with all other ingredients. Pour into an empty salt shaker.

Dulse Tonic: a remedy for the homesick Maritimer

Get in the habit of keeping Dulse Spice Blend on the table instead of high-salt commercial spice blends. Dulse Tonic is a soothing drink on a cold winter day or whenever you need to boost your mood or energy level. A quick way is to pour boiling water over a tea bag-size quantity of dulse with a dash of cayenne pepper. Drain and enjoy this broth of the sea. Some like it with a few drops of lime for extra zip. This is a satisfying drink, sure to warm up cold feet and hands. It is also known to relieve sinus troubles, but most of all it is a remedy for homesick Maritimers.

Dulse Vinaigrette. Dulse is an excellent replacement for salt, as it has trace vitamins and minerals.

Dulse Vinaigrette takes nothing more than adding shredded dulse to your favourite homemade vinaigrette instead of table salt. Dulse holds up very well in plant-based oils. Here is a simple homemade recipe that works well as a salad dressing or as a sauce for rice and pastas.

DULSE VINAIGRETTE

* 1 clove garlic
* 1 hard-boiled egg yolk (discard whites)
* 15 ml (1 tbsp) dijonnaise (or 7 ml [1/2 tbsp] each mayonnaise and mustard)
* 175 ml (3/4 cup) olive oil
* 15 ml (1 tbsp) lemon juice
* 60 ml (1/4 cup) shredded, rinsed dulse

1. Grate garlic finely. Crush the hard-boiled egg yolk into garlic with a few drops olive oil until a thick paste is achieved. Mix in prepared dijonnaise.

2. Slowly incorporate olive oil and continue stirring until vinaigrette is smooth. Add lemon juice.

3. Add dulse to mixture. Stir well.

Great served over salad greens, and also to flavour steamed rice or pasta. Will keep refrigerated for about three days.

9

The Coastal Vegetable Garden

In order to live off a garden, you practically have to live in it.
—Frank McKinney Hubbard—

Growing your own food is amazing, even if it is nothing more than a little patch of lettuce or potatoes or a row of onions. It is great to know exactly where your food came from and what went into its production. Growing edibles by the sea is essentially a metaphor for living. As with plants, we too have life phases: the spring of youth, adulthood summer, middle age autumn, and the senior phase of winter. Growing a vegetable garden brings a certain awareness and appreciation of the earth's tiniest life systems, which have a big impact on the overall health of food crops. The more I garden, the more I appreciate what went into growing a certain crop.

We pick and choose our days to look after the seaside vegetable garden. To tend a little garden is a practical way of staying active in the fresh air, with many returns. We learn as we go. Growing a vegetable garden is as cyclical as the phases of the moon; from seeds to plants, to the compost pile and back again to the soil. We waste nothing. When everything seems to be ready all at once, what we cannot use fast enough; we freeze, pickle, give away, feed to the goats, or—if overly ripe—return to the compost heap. Everything has a useful place.

The case has also been made for the benefits to the immune system from exposure to soil microbes from a young age. So parents and grandparents take heed: get the kids involved. Make growing food from the ground up with your young people your legacy.

Michael Opalka assists with harvesting garden-fresh cucumber

The creation story of the Garden of Eden as described in the book of Genesis is actually a food garden, specifically of fruit trees. Savouring a freshly picked, crisp apple while watching the sunrise over the ocean is nothing short of heaven. Imagine digging a hole in the ground and finding food! Imagine having fresh vegetables at arm's length. How thrilling it is to have a bounty of nourishment in one space; a place by the sea, where you can forage for the moment and collect your next meal directly, from vine to plate.

Cauliflower is not disturbed by a little flurry of snow.

Every garden plant is beautiful, and each one, without exception, produces something edible, nutritious, and delicious.... Paradise indeed.

The coastal vegetable garden does enjoy a few perks. We seaside gardeners could celebrate Thanksgiving holiday along with our American neighbours rather than the early October Canadian Thanksgiving weekend. While it is snowing in the Annapolis Valley today, here I am harvesting big, fat white onions, carrots, potatoes, and turnip well into December. Broccoli, cauliflower, and Brussels sprouts are able to endure a wet flurry or two.

Depending on the year, it is not inconceivable to have some tender vegetables holding up into late December. The row of salad greens I planted late summer is still producing crunchier-than-ever leaves with the aid of just a homemade mini greenhouse (see p. 134). The ground doesn't freeze significantly at the coast until mid-January. Parsley can be picked from under a layer of snow. Here, it comes back as a perennial. The ocean is slow to cool and keeps the atmosphere over our seaside gardens warmer for a longer period than inland areas. The sea acts as an air conditioning system, keeping air relatively cool and moist during summer months and milder during the cold winter months.

Tending a vegetable garden is not much different than keeping house.

LIKE GARDEN, LIKE HOUSE

There isn't much difference between tending a vegetable garden and keeping house. Domestic chores are just a matter of course to those of us who have a strong emotional attachment to our home. Growing a vegetable garden is not at all like a carpenter setting out to build a deck. The deck will endure for many years without touch-ups. The garden on the other hand, as with keeping house, requires ongoing attention. There are always chores to be done. As the house has to be cleared of dust bunnies, the vegetable garden must be cleared of weeds. If you absolutely abhor housework, then you may want to skip this chapter: starting a vegetable garden by the sea may not be for you. If you aren't sure, start slowly with just one or two items the first year and see how it goes.

The vegetable garden begins with spring cleaning. This takes place as soon as the days get significantly longer, the air a little warmer, when the ground can be worked. What sets gardening apart from the ho-hum tasks of household chores is that we gardeners get to be outside. We work the land along with chirping robins and song sparrows while watching colourful boats competing for the best spots to set lobster traps. Outside, we are in touch with the elements in their purest form: sea, sky, and soil. Here, no criticism comes to us for having untidy hair, soil under our fingernails, and knees caked in mud.

As with a house, the vegetable garden has many "rooms," each of which serves a particular function. Root vegetables are kept in a room where they will not disturb other crops when they are pulled up, and the surrounding soil needs to remain piled up to the vegetables' "ankles" to prevent sun damage. Perennials like asparagus, rhubarb, blueberries, and raspberries have their own room where no tilling takes place. Some rooms require high walls for climbing beans and peas to cling to. Other rooms are laid out to capture the most sunlight, alongside a few rooms for plants that are not so sun needy. Like a house, furniture and decor get moved around to suit the changing seasons.

Then there is the "laundry room." I am always picking up after the "kids" out here. By this I mean gathering spent plant material: dead flower heads, old stalks, thinnings, and stubborn weeds. The compost pile can be thought of as a big laundry basket that is perpetually topped, layer by layer, emptied, and layered again with plant waste. Unlike doing the laundry at home, composting is part of the grand cycle of nature I feel so fortunate to be a part of (see chapter 7). The rewards are well worth the extra effort.

The nice thing about raising plants is that they never talk back. The vegetable garden takes very well to a bit of discipline. Like parenting, to garden is to nurture and to steer your "kids" in the right direction. Tomatoes too tall? Clip their tops and they will widen. Basil getting too wide? Clip a few side branches and it will spurt upward. Plants too crowded? Dig them up and move them to a new part of the garden. Plants actually appreciate this kind of tough love.

Come fall, one by one, the "kids" begin to leave home. It is time to go through each room thoroughly to be sure nothing has been left behind. Once the soil is turned and raked over in preparation for new seeds, I stand back awhile. How gratifying. Room by room, the outdoor "house" becomes as clean as can be, the soil as fresh and as uniform as a new rug on the living room floor. I already anticipate the next generation of garden family life.

The vegetable garden is where I spend most of my gardening time. Although it is the most demanding of all my gardens, I don't mind since I get so much more than pretty flowers out of it. There is no denying that growing food takes work and time. But even when I was a full-time public schoolteacher, I felt it was time well spent. Granted, I had July and August free, but most of the hard labour takes place in April and May. After that, it is simply a matter of general upkeep and the pleasurable act of harvesting the goodness of the Earth. I actually like getting down and dirty when there is still a chill in the early spring air. Some people go to the gym to stay fit, I go to my vegetable garden with my pitchfork and shovel. It's a good, purposeful muscle and cardio workout. The fresh, salty spring air is a bonus, but the true reward is fresh, nutritious food that's as easy and convenient as going to the pantry.

Root vegetables do well at the coast, despite wind and salt spray.

AN OUTDOOR PANTRY BY THE SEA

Growing our own food is the ultimate way of eating seasonally and locally. Edibles can be grown just about anywhere that offers shelter from onshore winds. Each crop can have its own spot. Plantings do not necessarily have to be all under the same "roof." Look for little protected nooks and crannies that are easily accessible. Homeowners may not be able to grow everything needed to feed their family

A patch of Swiss chard grows in the protection of a seaside cottage

throughout the year, but you *can* grow a considerable amount of fresh fruit, vegetables, and culinary herbs all season. If space is limited, consider container gardening. All edibles, with the exception of root crops, can be grown in a regular plant pot. This offers the advantage of portability to a sheltered spot when salty winds threaten.

In addition to money and carbon footprint savings, homegrown food is enjoyed fresh as can be and at optimal time of ripeness. Supermarket fruit and vegetables are mass-produced primarily for appearance, size, speed of growth, and shelf life—not so much for nutrient content. Your market tomatoes, for example, have been picked pink and still green inside for transport. Just before arriving to their destination, a gas called ethylene is artificially released as a treatment to hasten ripening evenly. Those supermarket "on the vine" tomatoes are not vine-ripened. It's a marketing ploy.

Homegrown food, on the other hand, is tended with caring hands, on a small plot of compost-rich soil and minimal, if any, chemical residue. It sure beats the drive out to the supermarket, where much of the fresh produce appears to have been picked prematurely and its flavour is, more often than not, disappointing. Most have been shipped thousands of kilometres to market. Convenience? Not as convenient as a little skip to the backyard, as needed, with the luxury of harvesting just at mealtime, or for a spontaneous snack. This is even better than the 100-Mile Diet—this is the 0-mile diet! There is no necessity to keep produce refrigerated for a week or more. Have you ever found your purchase spoiled somewhere in the back corner of the refrigerator? Wouldn't it be

Young romaine lettuces offer their outer leaves as an early harvest from the outdoor pantry

nice to go straight to a well-stocked outdoor pantry for optimal freshness?

There is another concern when it comes to store-bought food: everything seems to be getting bigger these days. My homegrown strawberries may be small by comparison, but their taste is far superior to those imported from afar. Mine are red throughout, while supermarket strawberries are white inside and are either bland or tart to the taste. Growing my own food relieves many concerns I have about store-bought produce: How was it handled? Were hands well washed? Was irrigation water safe from E. coli? What kind of herbicides, pesticides, genetically engineered mutation, and artificial fertilizers have gone into producing this strawberry nearly the size of an apple?

Growing my own food gives me control over what goes into my "outdoor pantry." It is great to know exactly where my food came from and what went into its production. There is nothing tastier or more satisfying than enjoying the fruits of one's little labour of love, from pot to plate. The following recipe is one of our favourite easy, straight-from-the-garden lunches.

FRESH GARDEN VEGGIE ROLLS

Serves 2

A great way to celebrate eating wholesome, raw, fresh foods with a hint of the sea, this quick and simple Asian-style recipe is sure to be a hit.

- 1 cucumber, peeled, seeds removed, cut into narrow sticks
- 1/4 small onion, thinly sliced
- 1/2 carrot, julienned
- 250 ml (1 cup) prepared spinach rice (or plain) vermicelli, cooled to room temperature
- 3 sheets nori*
- 150 ml (3/4 cup) fresh chopped mint leaves

Fresh veggie rolls served with a side of shrimp celebrate the goodness of land and sea.

Dipping Sauce:

- 60 ml (1/4 cup) Asian fish sauce
- 5 ml (1 tsp) sugar
- dash cayenne pepper

1. Beginning at the bottom of 1 nori sheet, place garden veggies lengthwise beginning with cucumber, onion, and carrot. This should not take up more than 1/4 of 1 sheet of nori.

2. Arrange prepared noodles thinly over the rest of the nori sheet, bottom to top, leaving about 1 cm (1/4 in.) free. Wet this part of nori sheet with Dipping Sauce. Sprinkle chopped mint over noodles.

3. Roll sheet tightly, from the bottom up to where the section wetted with sauce will hold the roll together. Slice rolls in half and enjoy with Dipping Sauce. Goes well with a side of shrimp.

PLANT PROTECTION

Food crops are cultivated plants that are, by definition, domesticated. Just like the animals we have domesticated over many centuries, these plants can no longer fend for themselves in the great wilderness without human intervention. Their survival has become dependent on us. This is the legacy of the home vegetable gardener as well as industrial crop producers. The difference between the two is that I find myself, as a gardener, in the simple down-to-earth role of a sort of shepherd guarding a "small flock" of vegetables. There *are* predators to guard against, but they can be dealt with hands-on, without mass spraying against specialized pests. Here at the coast, our issues are minimal. They come in the form of just a few bugs, birds, deer, and, of course, the elements.

THE GOOD, THE BAD, AND THE UGLY CREATURES OF THE GARDEN

One thing we don't have control over in the garden is the insects that frequent our plants and soil. Bugs go hand in hand with gardening. Most are harmless, beneficial, or are essential pollinators. A pinch of fertile soil observed under the microscope reveals a myriad of bug-eat-bug communities too small for the naked eye to appreciate. The greater the activity, the greater is soil fertility. If it weren't for the bugs, the entire planet would be a sterile desert. While we don't tolerate them coming into our homes, we must have a different mindset about insects in the garden.

Even slugs play an important roll in breaking down organic material into nutrient-rich matter that plants can use. I do allow them to hang out in the compost pile and on the heap of grass clippings for this reason. Although slugs, snails, and caterpillars do serve a useful function in the grand scheme of things, we cannot ignore them when they eat the food that we have grown, oh no! There is plenty else out there for them to eat. I tell them, "You can partake of any part of this garden, as for this area: '*Thou shalt not eat of it: for in the day that thou shall eatest thereof, thou shalt surely die.*'" This is where I become "a real control freak," as my husband puts it.

Frogs are always welcome in the garden to keep bug population down.

Tent caterpillars retreat to their webby nests

One morning, while culling slugs and snails, I decided to inspect my young apple trees to see how their fruit was developing. To my horror I discovered the dreaded tent caterpillar. Panic set in at the thought of a population explosion. My trees were too young to survive the magnitude of such an attack. Immediate removal was my first instinct—but how? There were so many.

Fortunately, come midday, they move to their webby tents in tight clusters. From a stepladder, I promptly removed the affected branches and put them in a five-gallon bucket filled with seawater. *That should take care of them*, I thought, *and then they can be thrown to sea for fish food....* Nope. They floated to the surface and began their journey down the sides of the bucket. I tried stepping on them (X%*≠@%&*≠!); there were too many. My stomach couldn't handle it. I then got a big garbage bag and put the creepy-crawly branches inside, one by one, double-bagged them tightly, and put them in the garbage can. No air, no daylight, no water, no food. Done!

On garbage day two days later, my husband went to the garage to get the can for curbside pickup. When he opened the door, it snowed caterpillars. "Come see this!" he shouted. The garage door, windows, walls, and ceiling were black with tent caterpillars. They clung to each other like dripping Velcro! The garbage can was so covered it was barely recognizable. Well, I had some explaining to do. The caterpillars had all hatched, chewed their way out of plastic, and wanted out. The garbage can lid must have been just loose enough for them to escape. To make a long story short, we were not about to let them get outside. We closed the garage door and waited for a mass die-off to take place (about four days) and then sucked the carnage up with the Shop-Vac.

I wish now, in retrospect, that I had taken a photo of this extreme event for the book. I remember thinking at the time that I would be putting my ignorance on display. I know better now what to do with an army of threatening bugs. Since that episode, whenever I discover insect-covered branches, I roll the affected branches in newspaper and set them ablaze in the fire pit. Eradication is instant.

Unfortunately, pests are a reality in the garden. But don't give up the ship so soon. Remember that we coastal gardeners are spared from the worst. Gardening here is not done on a monocultural or industrial scale, so we are (usually) far removed from such practices that breed insect specialists. As an example, for all the spuds that I grow, I have never seen a potato bug, but have seen their devastating effects on inland crops. Vigilance is key. Do daily inspections to catch problems early before they get a chance to fester.

I have come up with a few strategies for keeping the most annoying seaside garden pests at bay. Most Maritime gardeners will point to slugs, deer, and ants as being the most problematic. Deterring them from entering the garden in the first place is always the best strategy.

SEASIDE SNAIL AND SLUG SOLUTIONS

The worst garden pest of all is the sneaky, squalid, nocturnal slug. Slugs and snails are impervious to any kind of barrier, except seaweed. Seaweed application is a brilliant, organic way to deter slugs and snails from settling comfortably in your vegetable garden. Have you ever seen a slug at the beach sucking on seaweed? They recoil in its presence. Fresh or dried, slugs and snails snub seaweed. As soon as they encounter it, they turn the other way. If you have access to plenty of seaweed, line the perimeter of your garden with it. A sea plant called knotted wrack makes an attractive black mulch with the added benefit of adding nutrients to the soil (see p. 108). When applied around vulnerable young plants and flower beds, an environment most uninviting to slugs is created. Slugs need dark, damp places to shelter from sun and to reproduce. Between my garden rows I use wooden planks salvaged from construction sites to keep weeding down, but it is a haven for slugs to hide.

Before putting planks down between rows in the vegetable garden, I line the furrow with a layer of rain-rinsed seaweed to keep the slugs from making their under-plank residence. This definitely puts a dent in the population! Planks are not necessary. Plain ol' seaweed between the rows will keep slugs out, but it can be unpleasant to walk on when wet. Seaweed can also be a good weed suppressant if at least .305 m (1 ft.) deep—if any shallower, weeds will happily come through. Now and then, despite all these efforts, I do come across a roaming slug. It sounds ruthless, but I do not hesitate snipping them

Planks over seaweed not only deter slugs and snails, but also eliminate the need to weed between the rows. They are also a nice, secure walking surface.

Old reclaimed bricks set down on compacted gravel (no mortar)

in two with scissors. Their little nutrient-rich bodies are then left to break down and become part of the soil's microbial community.

Slugs relish the same plants we do. In my own garden, I discovered that they had become well established between the bricks of the walkway in the fenced-in area of the garden. So again, I lined the inside of the raised beds with seaweed as a natural deterrent. The adults stay out but the nearly invisible maggot-sized slugs and snails are able to sneak under. They are too small to get with scissors, so additional measures are called for. As a rule, I abstain from any kind of chemical insecticide. But in this case, I can, in good conscience, apply slug-bait pellets to the gaps between bricks. Knowing that the poison would not be in contact with garden soil, beneficial frogs or birds, eases my conscience. Tiny slugs and snails snack on the bait before they get a chance to slither up the wooden raised beds. I find this works really well.

DEER DETERRENTS

The most common gardening question I get from gardeners is how to deal with deer. I have come to learn that there is no such thing as a deer-proof garden. I sarcastically say that I plant a row for us, and a row for them. I enjoy seeing deer and don't wish to harm them. But here is an interesting discovery: the aroma of poppies is offensive to deer. We have observed them circle the garden, heads low, tails down, and then quietly walk away when our annual poppies are in bloom. So you will see attractive volunteer poppy flowers left

Deer often travel in herds. Unprotected garden favourites can be decimated overnight.

The scent of poppies in bloom will turn deer away.

to grow, casually, here and there, throughout our veggie garden.

Poppy seedpods are easy to collect (see p. 53), and one pod will do for the entire garden. Starting in May, I gently shake the pod where I would like to see poppies come up. I do this every two weeks for successive blooms. Be sure to pull the plants up after flowering so that the soil doesn't get full of seeds. The entire plant can go on the compost pile as long as the pods are still green.

This may surprise some gardeners, but deer *do* have a discerning palate. They are as fussy as two-year-olds. So I grow their favourite snacks inside a chicken wire fence and the rest of my plants outside of it, within the privet windscreen. Here is what deer would devour to the ground given a chance: all manner of peas, beans, and tomatoes. That's about it! It is surprising that the deer don't wipe out the salad bar row that is kept outside the chicken wire fence. They do nibble here and there, but lettuce grows back in no time. I have never lost a carrot, only part of the green tops. As for the rest, the worst that happens is a few crops get trampled on. This is a minor irritant that I can live with.

Since there are only a handful of plants that are absolutely irresistible to deer, I am able to keep the wire enclosure small, affordable, and visually pleasing. I can easily see through it to the ocean and the material makes a great support for climbers, like scarlet runner and my beloved morning glory vines. Deer delicacies are grown in raised wooden beds with old salvaged bricks as walking paths between the cribs, over gravel for good drainage. No mortar is used (p. 128). The deer could jump the chest-high, see-through wire enclosure, but landing on brick between cribs is nerve-wracking to them. I don't get one or two deer here, I have been visited by a herd of as many as eight. They circle the enclosure but have never broken in—except when I forgot to close the gate!

Deer like to know they will land safely when jumping over a structure. They also need space to gather momentum for the leap, especially over a wide enclosure like a hedge (see Wise Windbreaks, p. 133). Another deer deterrent to is to use planks between the rows inside the walls of a "green fence." Deer instinctively know that their weight could shift the planks upon landing, which could cause them to lose their footing. Old reclaimed planks offer the additional benefit of reducing the need to weed, conserve moisture, and, when placed over seaweed, leave slugs nowhere to hide from the sun.

A bountiful harvest, free of deer nibbles

A large outdoor dog housed near the garden overnight is most definitely disruptive to a deer's enjoyment of your plants. Electric fences are a popular and effective deer deterrent if there is an easy access to a power source. It only needs to be turned on during night hours. However, a live electric line does not keep smaller creatures like rabbits and gophers out. There are many home solutions rumoured to work if you don't mind the look of them: clanging aluminum pie plates, installing red reflectors, hanging old CDs, bright markers, soap bars, the list goes on.

Finally, for gardeners who want but a small patch of peas and beans, there is an easy and simple alternative to electric wires and fences: retired lobster traps! Mine appeared above the high-water mark following a storm. When used in the garden, they restrict access

No bird, gopher, rabbit, porcupine, or deer can access these delectable bush beans—only you!

not only to deer but also to birds, snowshoe hares, and gophers. Robins and starlings are notorious for pulling young bean sprouts out of the ground, perhaps because they resemble yummy worms. These wire mesh "boxes" come with a convenient lobster-removal lid at the top and two round openings at the sides for easy access to the bush beans, while protecting them from predators. It doesn't get more nautical than that!

HOW TO SET UP A LOBSTER-TRAP GARDEN

Step 1: Spread a thick-gauge landscaping tarp the size of your lobster trap base over rich, cultivated soil for a weed-free garden.

Step 2: Place reclaimed wire mesh traps over the tarp.

Step 3: Cut off excess rope and twine from wire traps.

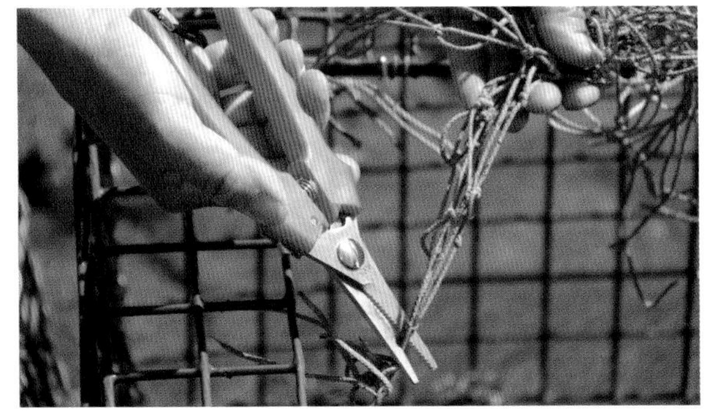

Step 4: Using tape, mark no more than six planting spots per trap.

Step 5: Remove traps from marked tarp.

Step 6: Make incisions into tarp and plant two seeds in each opening. Place trap over tarp. Thin to the strongest seedling.

Enjoy the bountiful harvest!

ANTS IN THE PLANTS

Ants actually provide the Earth with a great service: they aerate soil very efficiently and help to decompose organic materials. Now and then, however, ants decide to set up camp in garden spaces that we, and our plants, occupy. The most disturbing issue I have had with ants took place the year I grew a spectacular patch of dwarf sunflowers by the sea.

The soil was rather sandy. I noticed individual flowers folding over. Upon close inspection, I discovered that the stems had what looked like cuts, like those a chainsaw would make in the trunk of a tree.

Although good for aeration and composting, a colony of ants can cause unsightly blemishes to the gardenscape.

Shake cornmeal over ant-infested areas

Dozens of ants were travelling back and forth between these incisions and the ground. They had apparently found a spot of entry and were busily harvesting their "sweet" prize. Although I was very annoyed at this sight, there wasn't much I could do about it. I refuse to use chemical solutions directly in my gardens. Boiling water works for an infestation in the lawn, but in this case the flower bed was too large and the ants were too spread out. Scalding the beloved sunflowers that I had grown from seed was not an option.

My non-chemical solution to this ant problem was discovered quite accidently. About a week afterwards, I noticed that the left side of the sunflower garden had ceased losing its flowers—their injuries had healed over and the ants were gone—but the right side was still very much affected. What was the difference? On my knees, poking around the soil, I noticed only one difference between the right and left side. Just a week before, the committed composter that I am had decided to discard a bag of stale cornmeal over the soil on the left side of the flower bed for the birds. Could it be that this made ants sick? Could it be that they were unable to digest it?

I thought it would be worth the investment to throw some more cornmeal where ants were still active. Sure enough, the problem came to a halt in about a week. I have since tried it in other gardens. Fellow gardeners tell me that it has worked wonders. We think that it may depend on ant species, though. This is a solution deserving further study. To my surprise, when I queried this problem online, I discovered that I am not alone! This site offered the best theories into why cornmeal may get rid of an ant problem: www.ehow.com/info_8243816_cornmeal-really-kill-ants.html.

Another solution is to create a scent barrier at the location of infestation. Ants going up and down the trunk of a tree, for instance, follow a chemical scent to their destination. Choose a time when no rain is forecast for most of the week. Confuse the ants by surrounding the base of the tree with grated citrus rind. Then smear the trunk of the tree with pureed fresh onions. This will not kill them, but after three or four days, the ants will move elsewhere—hopefully away from the garden.

The best approach is a preventative one: plant in soil that is unappealing to ants. Some seaside soils can be very sandy, which is an ideal environment for ant nests. So dig lots of compost in before you plant. Soil rich in organic material is ideal for plants, not so much for ants.

This gardener has a novel way of protecting the garden from wind and salt spray.

WISE WINDBREAKS

The greatest discouragement to gardening at the coast is the wind and salt spray that goes with it. Without some protection, seaborne winds can scorch and flatten crops in a matter of hours. There are many common sense solutions, such as growing against or near a structure in the wind's path, but some seasoned seaside gardeners have come up with ingenious ways to address these issues. I couldn't resist taking a photo of this firewood windbreak, which includes a window to the sea. This is brilliant because the "green" wood needs to be piled to air and cure before it can be burned for heating. By the time firewood is needed, the garden has been put to rest for winter.

The problem with being a visual person is that artistry, even in the vegetable garden, is high on my agenda. This space has to feel inviting for me to want to spend time in there. So, for that reason, I favour a "living windscreen" to reduce wind force instead of a solid fence. Here are some reasons why: A high wall, although an efficient wind guard, will cast shade on the sun-needy plants and I don't particularly like feeling barricaded. Scraping old paint, repainting, and having to replace a wooden structure every few years are not, to me, time and money well spent.

What I mean by a "living windscreen" is any chest-high, densely planted hedge. There are several available hedge plants hardy to zone 4—your safest sea/garden barrier. Many shrubs can serve as a hedge when planted side by side and relatively close. Yew, forsythia, spiraea, and juniper are good candidates, but shrubs are pricey and some take nearly a decade to fill out. Native spruce makes an excellent wind barrier, but again, it takes it a few years to fill out and must be kept short by regular pruning.

Free-growing privet hugs the garden and shields it against fierce, northern ocean winds.

My windscreen is simply privet. The small, thick leaves and stiff woody stems of this shrub tolerate sea situations well. Planted 60 cm (2 ft.) apart, it is fast growing, relatively inexpensive, and easy to plant (mine came in bundles of ten, no pots). The first year, deer could still walk through but would not eat it. Deer do not like privet! By year two, the hedge was 1 m (3 ft.) high, dense and thick enough that deer felt blocked out. Year four, it had reached its unkept peak of height—a good 2 m (about 7 ft). Ideally you want wind protection on at least two sides of the produce garden: on the water side and on the north side where winds are coldest.

A living windscreen of coastal forest or coastal vegetation between the sea and the garden is an excellent way to keep salt spray and wind from reaching it. If wind from the water is not so much of a threat, one can leave that side of the garden open but keep trees for shelter from brisk winds coming from other directions.

Just a few dense conifers in the path of the sea will break down wind and salt spray efficiently.

EXTENDING THE SEASON: HOMEMADE MINI GREENHOUSE

The best way to extend the growing season by the sea on both ends, very early spring and then very late fall, is to have a little greenhouse. Maritime spring at the coast can be particularly unforgiving to young plants. But with the aid of a mini greenhouse, transplanting salad greens, cold-tolerant vegetables, and herbs can begin as soon as April. A mini greenhouse can also keep your coastal harvest going well into late December. The plants just need a bit of shelter for an early start, and again late in the season to keep going.

A greenhouse is basically a structure that traps solar heat and light, while insulating plants from harsh winds and frost. The trouble with a walk-in, fixed greenhouse is that, unless growing specialty tomatoes, peppers, and cucumbers that require tropical conditions, this structure is no longer necessary from mid-June to mid-October—our entire outdoor

A mini greenhouse allows a crop of romaine lettuce leaves to be harvested as early as April.

The mini greenhouse keeps a sudden May frost from damaging the early romaine lettuce.

growing season! Since you won't have any reason to be in there, the structure will end up standing empty, neglected, and tend to get stubborn molds once plants have been moved outside. Plants kept in a sheltered environment cannot develop resilience to the elements. They wilt at the slightest change of atmosphere. Furthermore, unless you have some sort of irrigation and ventilation system, the heat from the high noon sun coming into a walk-in greenhouse can potentially bake young crops. Finally, there is a cost associated with ventilating a walk-in greenhouse, while what comes from outside is free.

Plants need to be introduced to the great outdoors early in their stage of growth in order to build strong "bones," but gently and gradually (see "Hardening off Seedlings for the Seaside Garden," p. 50). Most don't like to be transplanted or dug up. Ideally, it would be preferable to somehow be able to lift the roof off of the greenhouse during sunny days, put it back on at night and be put away all together for the regular growing season. The great advantage of my portable mini greenhouse is that you can place it where it is needed, when it is needed. The top can slide up for ventilation or be taken off altogether on warmer days. Furthermore, this little unit folds up for easy, inconspicuous storage, which happens to be during most of the growing season. A real space saver!

Thanks to my not only portable, but also collapsible, mini greenhouse, my family is still enjoying a variety of fresh, crunchy lettuces, spinach, cilantro, and arugula in the third week of December. During those frigid spells when the weather forecasted is below 10 degrees Celsius (50 degrees Fahrenheit), I simply throw an old blanket over my mini greenhouse for an extra measure of protection.

Many more edibles can be extended into the "cold season" at the coast. Swiss chard and crucifers like broccoli, cauliflower, Brussels sprouts, and endives are all easy-to-grow fall-to-late-December crops at the coast. When more than 5 cm (2 in.) of snow is scheduled to come down, I place one of my mini greenhouses over them to ensure harvest for a little longer. Although the hours of direct sunlight are greatly reduced at this time of year, what does reach the plants is intensified because of the mini "greenhouse effect." Those few hours of super sunshine warm the soil enough to withstand the cold coming at it from the outside, even at night. Under the protection of a mini greenhouse, early spring and late fall frosts and flurries do not affect plant performance.

A Plexiglas mini greenhouse is very durable. This one has been in use for fifteen years. A piece of driftwood keeps the lid up on warm, sunny days.

Late crops should be started early to mid-August, directly in the garden. Come October, when the possibility of frost is imminent, out comes my portable mini greenhouse. I place it over the young plants that will continue to contribute to the kitchen for several more weeks with a little protection. I can't help but brag about the virtues of picking fresh, bug- and weed-free salad greens and herbs mid- to late December. To my eye, this is both a more attractive and efficient intervention than plastic sheets over hoops, which sag under rain and snow. If you live on the water, the plastic often flies off the hoops out to sea, a very distressing sight. Removal and storage is also a pain with plastic, whereas my portable mini greenhouse is almost as easy to install and remove as flicking on a light switch. The first one I built, about fifteen years ago, is still in full use. I've found it so beneficial that I have since built three more.

No tools or special skills are necessary to build this little kit. It is easily moved around the garden as needs arise. The plants stay put. The mini greenhouses, on the other hand, get moved around. The benefit of having a relatively small greenhouse is that the soil temperature, like the ocean, regulates the atmosphere. It is able to moderate extremes in heat and cold from dusk to dawn. You don't get that massive heat buildup of a walk-in-size greenhouse. A knee-high mini greenhouse is in enough proximity to the cool soil to create a perfect plant-friendly climate. The lid slides up to allow a gentle breeze in, allowing plants to gradually acclimatize to the elements.

Duct tape both sides of the seams where the pieces join.

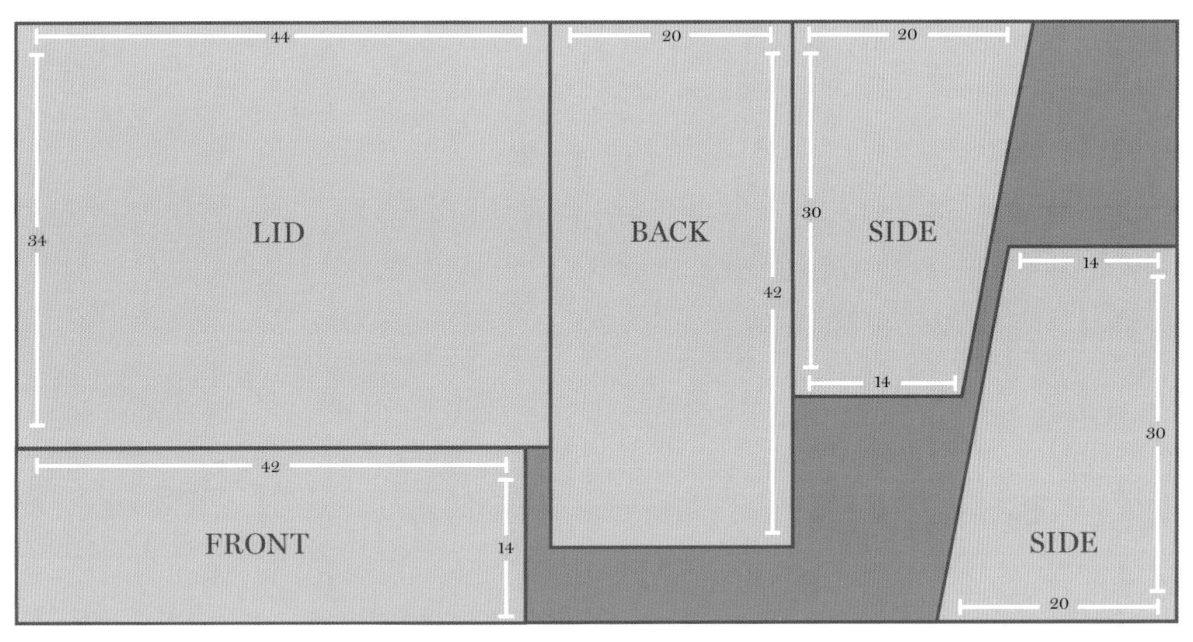

How to get the most out of a 1/4 in. thick, 4 x 8 ft. wide sheet of Plexiglas.

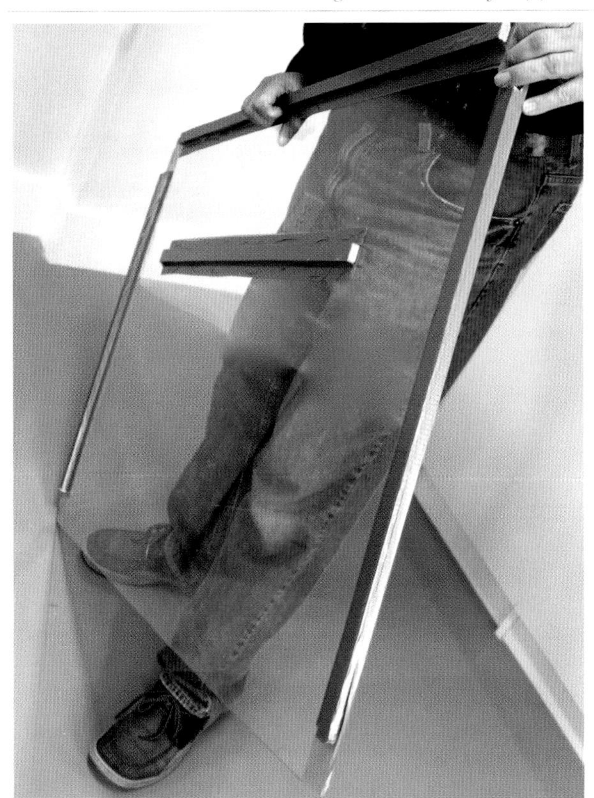

To slide up and down, a stick or two taped on the lid will serve as a stopper, allowing airflow on warm days.

BUILDING YOUR OWN PORTABLE MINI GREENHOUSE

All you need is a 4 x 8 ft., 1/4 in.-thick sheet of Plexiglas and a roll of duct tape. Most hardware stores provide a cutting service. Above you'll find the most efficient cuts you can get from a 4 x 8 ft. sheet.

Step 1: Peel the protective blue plastic coating off each cut.

Step 2: Place pieces, two at a time, in their collapsed position to tape them together.

Step 3: Double tape each seam, inside and out, for durability.

Step 4: The lid should stand alone. Tape narrow sticks along the top and two sides.

Step 5: Tape additional sticks midway to slide lid up and allow for ventilation.

A few planks placed near the mini greenhouse extend its use. Here it protects an ealy April crop of herbs.

Temporary extensions can be easily added to the mini greenhouse to offer additional protection to nearby plants. In this case, I was able to keep cilantro going well into December by simply resting old windowpanes over the top of the mini greenhouse on one end, and over old wooden planks on the other, with my favourite herb protected in between.

FOG-LOVING CROPS

Root vegetables thrive in the Atlantic coastal climate. Their moisture-rich foot in the ground is a reserve of energy unaffected by salty air. In fact, potatoes, turnips, and carrots prefer slightly acidic soil and moist, cool air. I must give special mention to my favourite (dietician-recommended) potato: the red-skinned Chieftain. It is attractive, low in starch, and

A fog-loving carrot as big as my head!

Chieftains are lower in starch than other potato varieties.

All brassicas, broccoli included, thrive at the coast and suffer little insect damage.

Coastal Water Conservation Tip

Cucumbers and tomatoes rinsed in sea water

Washing the soil and debris off crops can use up a lot of valuable fresh water. Many coastal homes are on a cistern system (either rainwater collection or imported town water). A first measure of conservation is to first shake or roll vegetables and root crops over a grassy area to remove the bulk of soil. This way, valuable soil is returned to the ground where it belongs. With most of the soil removed, take the harvest to the shore for a good rinse at sea. Seaweed is great for removing the remaining dirt and potential bugs hanging on for dear life. Salt water shocks insects and they promptly let go. If your produce is going to be stored a few days in the refrigerator, give it a quick rinse in fresh water. Otherwise, consider sea-washed lettuces, cucumbers, and tomatoes ready to eat: they are already salty from the soak. Just add a bit of olive oil and a squeeze of lemon for a fresh, tasty, crunchy salad.

very versatile. Onion and garlic also do very well by the sea, as the soil here tends to contain a good supply of natural sulfur, which they need to thrive.

Broccoli, with its wide, water-filled girth, also thrives in cool, salty, damp air. This favourite, along with other popular brassicas like kale, cauliflower, Brussels sprouts, and cabbage, is prone to cabbageworm, a caterpillar the same colour as its host plant, making it difficult to detect before damage has taken place. There are organic bacteria-based sprays available to deter them, but I prefer to keep the egg layer—a butterfly commonly known as whitefly—out by simply keeping the crops covered in a light mesh from mid-June to late July (cheesecloth works well). This prevents them from accessing the underside of the fleshy leaves. Another solution is to plant brassicas in very early spring, before the whitefly arrives, or in September when the insect no longer is around. Keep broccoli going until it succumbs to a deep frost. It is extremely resilient. Even once florets have been cut off, it keeps producing a multitude of tasty little side shoots, well into the first few weeks of snowfall.

Salad greens, too, thrive in this cool, foggy climate. They stay crunchy, mild, and bug-free. Thanks to cool summers and foggy days, lettuce greens are less likely to bolt prematurely. Celery is another fog-loving crop. Its water-filled stalks do extremely well at the coast. It thrives in cool, hard rains, is super crunchy, and even tastes a little salty when grown by the sea.

Flavourful ground cherries come in fun little paper wraps. Kids love them!

TRY SOMETHING NEW

Every year I try something new; it keeps the romance alive. Children and guests will love these two: ground cherries and sunberries are both thriving annuals at the coast. Ground cherry fruit comes in fun little paper wraps, like a fortune cookie but with a sweet, pineapple-flavoured, golden berry inside. Visiting kids describe sunberries as tasting like Diet Coke: interesting, mildly sweet, and black. That deer don't care for either is a bonus.

Edamame, a soybean plant adapted to cool climates, is a new addition to regional seed catalogues.

This year, I tried growing a special heavy-yielding variety of edamame—it is in fact a fresh soybean—suited for cool conditions. Most regional seed

Coastal Tip

Rinsing vegetables at sea is an enjoyable task for kids. This is a fun and useful way to keep them active and involved in home-grown food.

Avery Opalka rinses freshly picked carrots in sea water

catalogues now offer a variety developed for our East Coast climate. The plant looks much like your regular garden-variety bush bean plant, but a bit fuzzier. Steamed and served shelled like regular fresh green peas, they are lovely and unique. Even my husband, the carnivore in the family, loves them with a bit of sea salt and butter (he doesn't know that they're soybeans).

Cinnamon the goat has a face that could sink a ship.

A SEASIDE HOBBY FARM:
PETER AND MARILYN CORKUM

It isn't often that one sees a cow foraging just above the high-water mark here in St. Margarets Bay. Recreational boaters are taken by surprise as they pass by, slowing down to have a better look at Buttercup, the Corkums' family pet, among other animals. The four-hectare (ten acre) hobby farm has been in Peter Corkum's family since 1944. His parents, Henry and Mary Corkum, built the original seaside cottage in this lovely, sheltered, sandy cove. Keeping a vegetable garden was a regular part of life in those days, and Mary always enjoyed the company of a few farm animals. This property was, and still is, an ideal spot for family members to get together over the summer months.

Buttercup, the seaside pet cow

Healthy animals and gardens by the sea

Today, Peter and his wife Marilyn continue the tradition of sharing the gifts of land and sea with their extended family. Their grandchildren look forward to reuniting with the animals they have named.

Enough produce to feed an army

Warm summer days are spent petting and feeding Buttercup the black cow, as well as rabbits and goats. They enjoy regular visits to their various breeds of poultry, including turkeys. They run between beach, garden, and animal husbandry all day while snacking on garden goodies—oh, the raspberries here! Just a hop, skip, and jump to other side of the cottage, tucked behind Peter's impressive vegetable gardens, are the pens that house not only rabbits and chickens, but several species of exotic pheasants, including peacocks. From dusk to dawn, there is always something going on here to wow the kids.

Peter runs a tight ship. He keeps a detailed timetable of what needs to be planted and when. He also uses a calendar to track which days the animals are due to give birth. Everything runs in cycles here. Peter is a real back-to-the-land type. The garden crops are

Peter's row plantings at different stages of production

grown out of the native soil. Over the decades, Peter and the generation before him have enriched it with compost made from nothing other than what his property yields naturally: seaweed, plant-based yard waste, and bedding material from his animal pens.

One of Peter's compost retainer systems

Peter has also devised a simple but brilliant composting system. As the compost pile grows, wooden planks are stacked on their sides, lengthwise, around it, to keep it contained. At the end of each growing season, Peter removes the planks to access the nutrient-rich compost, which he then incorporates into the soil just in time for the new growing season. Every fall, after the harvest, he works this rich compost into the soil, allowing the micro-organisms to replenish what was taken up by the crops. The following spring, the soil harbours a wealth of biological activity that provides everything any plant needs to thrive. Healthy plants mean healthy food at the picnic table!

10

Herbs for the Coastal Garden

Much virtue in herbs, little in men.
—Benjamin Franklin—

One can never be overly romantic about having herbs by the sea. There is something magical about stepping out in a cool ocean breeze to collect a handful of plants that will elevate the most mundane meal to the status of high cuisine with just a few sprigs and sprinkles. Depending on the plant, an herb's virtues can be derived from its root, stem, leaves, flowers, or seeds. The purpose of growing herbs, however, goes far beyond the role they play in the kitchen. Some herbs are used for their appeal as garnish, for their aroma, or use in teas and tonics, and others for their medicinal properties. Many herbs have more than one use while some are purely decorative, but, collectively, these are all plants with a legacy in the human quest for improving our quality of life. Herbs come with a long history, often surrounded by myth and folklore. I will be sharing a few of those stories and why I so value having herbs around me. They have taught me much about gardening by the sea.

A self-seeded patch of chamomile survives brutal winds and salt spray just fine.

HERBS THAT DO WELL AT THE COAST, AND HERBS THAT DON'T

Herbs are the most versatile plants in the seaside garden, and among the most robust. For the purpose of this book I will highlight those I have found to grow particularly well on the ocean side of our property and those favourites of mine that need a bit of shelter. Not all herbs are able to withstand the seaside climate. Some are too delicate. Perennial herbs are excellent candidates to grow close to the sea (I will explain why later in this chapter). Annuals, on the other hand, tend to prefer warmer climates. So I grow basil, rosemary, dill, and fennel in the protection of the vegetable garden on the lee side of the yard. Arugula, coriander, borage, parsley, and chamomile are the exception to the rule. These annuals do surprisingly well at the coast, as they are cold tolerant. They respond to windy conditions by staying relatively short, and grow dense roots to keep a firm footing.

Growing herbs in the path of the elements was not at all in the plans when I got started with seaside gardening. I usually like to keep edible plants all in one area: the vegetable garden, which is on the lee side of the property. However, some perennial herbs became far too aggressive for the vegetable garden. Like spoiled children, they were getting their way and stressing me out. What began as a clump of chives that I could hold in one hand turned into a patch nearly the size of a doormat the following year. Several times during the growing season I found myself digging up large amounts to make room for other plants. My lovely little knee-high lovage rapidly grew into a bush almost as tall as me and as wide as a refrigerator. Mint crawled every which way like a sneaky underground serpent. The creeping thyme spread into other rows like a bad rash. And then there was the oregano. It managed to spill over into the compost pile, where it grew so exponentially that it became difficult to avoid introducing it to new parts of the garden every time the compost was used. Beebalm and lemon balm, too, misbehaved. Like mint, they popped up uninvited in every direction among nearby vegetables.

Beebalm blossoms are a long-lived, fragrant hummingbird favourite.

As much as I love these perennial favourites, they had it too good. I had to put some restrictions on their unruly behaviour once and for all. But what kind of tough love could a gardener come up with besides total eradication? I resolved that these plants were too healthy in the vegetable garden, and that is when the idea of transplanting them near the sea, almost at water's edge, came about. I'd keep them in line by subjecting them to a bit of "seaside stress."

THE BENEFITS OF SEASIDE STRESS

Lovage was the first herb I moved to the ocean side of the property as an experiment. While it is not an invasive plant, when grown in very fertile soil it turns into an overly tall, gangly bush that casts shade on other, sun-needy vegetables (and I just don't use that much of it). It felt bad to do this, but I had to sheer my lovage plant down to the ground for the well-being of its neighbours. I didn't want to lose it altogether, but it had to come out of the vegetable garden. I walked around looking for a new place to move it. I like lovage enough that it would be nice to have it by the kitchen door, but I feared it would turn into a huge bush again. So I decided to move the lovage root right up to the shore, just above the high-water mark.

I started digging at it (and digging, and digging) and found myself hurling profanities at a plant! By the time my husband and I were done, it was so mangled I really didn't think that it stood a chance of surviving. In went a pathetic section of the huge lovage root ball.

The flavour of lovage is enhanced when grown close to the sea.

"That is where you go!" I told it. "There! Right at water's edge by the sea! You can grow as big as you want or you can die. If you don't make it, fine! I can always have celery leaves instead." I was so frustrated by its size and the work it took two of us to dig it up, that by then, I hoped my lovage would die.

It was early spring and the ground frost had just lifted. The seaside conditions were fierce that spring. There was no sign of life when I checked on the plant in May. I resolved that it had succumbed to the salt spray and poor soil conditions. I then forgot all about it, until something caught my eye during a stroll along the shore mid-June. There she was, a perky, fragrant, knee-high beauty. I am pleased to report that my resurrected lovage has maintained her modest body mass index ever since. It is just the right size for my cooking needs.

This experiment prompted me to plant a little herb garden by the sea, close to the kitchen door. *Yes*, I thought, *a little seaside stress is just what tyrant herbs need to be kept in check*. Also, by growing herbs close to the kitchen, they get used much more often during

Seaside chives in bloom

Chives are a staple, ready for use as garnish or flavouring from April to December at the coast.

food preparation than they would if grown further away. I wouldn't bother venturing out to a vegetable garden in another part of the yard to harvest them during cold, windy, or rainy days. And now that they are in a well-lit area by the kitchen door, my culinary herbs are easily accessible even after dark.

Herbs have an ornamental quality, so planting them on the sunny, ocean side of the house makes for an elegant but tame kitchen garden. Chives are especially appreciated for their lovely lavender blooms. Although nearly flattened when strong onshore winds hit, it is remarkable how quickly this plant rebounds once the wind has settled down. This lowly common herb is a staple in many kitchens. Its sweet, mild onion notes are tremendously versatile. Use it in soups, rice, sandwiches, seafood, potatoes, pasta, and meat dishes. Not only do chives enhance the flavour and aroma of a dish, they make an appetizing garnish as long, slender, tender stems casually dropped over lobster or chopped into tiny, tasty, hollow cylinders over a favourite side dish.

THE VIRTUES OF SEASIDE HERBS

The definition of "herb" is loose. In general, it is a plant's seed, roots, leaves, and/or flowers that serves a valuable function. There are also strong cultural ties to what is considered an herb. As an example, one of the most noxious, invasive plants in Maritime gardens is a prehistoric-looking plant we call "horsetail." But to pioneers it was considered an herb. Although it is the bane of many gardeners today, early settlers found its

SEASIDE SUGGESTION

When chives are in bloom, or better yet, still at the flower bud stage, cut them close to the base and pull them out from a handful of chive greens. The blooms make great everlasting arrangements. Fasten them together at the base with an elastic band. Leave chive flowers to dry on a windowsill overlooking the sea or hang them upside down until dry, when they will be rigid enough to stay upright.

Freshly picked chive buds hang to dry

Wild caraway growing at water's edge

silica, which act as bristles, to be superbly useful for polishing pewter, scrubbing out buckets, and scouring pots and pans. Another example is sorrel. A little "weed" with a pickle flavour that grows happily in our lawns and gardens. To those who appreciate it, it is an herb. But to those not wanting them on the lawn, it is definitely regarded as a weed. The perception of a plant as an herb is subjective. One gardener's herb may very well be another gardener's weed.

NATIVE AND NATURALIZED HERBS AT THE COAST

There are a few lesser-known native and naturalized herbs that grow well in coastal areas that are deserving of special mention. Here are a few that frequent Maritime shores:

Caraway is a garden escapee that grows quite happily along seaside roadways. It is always a pleasant discovery to come upon it. Caraway seeds are useful for pickling or adding to mild cheeses and gourmet breads. Its unique flavor is reminiscent of mint with a tangy, peppery aftertaste.

Wintergreen, a common, low-growing plant, also thrives among the mosses of Maritime coastal forests and bogs. Its bright red berries, a cross between apple and mint, are a great breath freshener. Its leaves are often used in specialty teas. Steep them fresh or dried

Wintergreen plants are a common sight in coastal forests and bogs.

as you would any other tea and enjoy its classic flavour and aroma. Nowadays, the taste of wintergreen is produced synthetically to flavour candies, mints, chewing gum, toothpaste, and medicinal syrups. However, using the real thing is so much better for its added benefit of vitamin C and antioxidants. A drink of simmered, crushed wintergreen berries makes a soothing tonic for sore throats.

Orache, also known as "lamb's quarters," is a wild plant that thrives at the coast and in unmanaged meadows. Its tender leaves make a delightful addition to salads and soups. If you find it growing on a beach, it will taste slightly salty with a hint of earthy nuttiness.

The hop plant is a tenacious, fast-growing, perennial vine, which makes it a good candidate for seaside gardens. It thrives at the coast, even among native plants. I discovered it naturalized on our property over an old stone wall dating back to the 1800s. Hops die back completely at the end of the growing season. Come spring, they come up as little shoots resembling miniature asparagus. Traditionally used as a preservative in beer, young hop sprigs can be cooked and eaten just as you would eat asparagus—that is if you don't mind a slightly bitter aftertaste.

Violas of various kinds pop up in new places every spring. Locals call them "lady lights."

Hops are a fast-growing decorative vine. Cut them back to the ground when leaves have dropped for a new spring display.

Little Johnny jump ups are another viola that appear here and there in the garden and in the lawn. They are so common that some gardeners regard them as a weed. Their delicate blossoms make a lovely garnish on any dish or floating over a cold summer drink.

In short, an herb can be any plant that provides a service. Those with broad leaves, like nasturtiums, cranesbill, and lady's mantel are usually grown for their colourful blooms but can also serve as weed suppressants between perennials. Another beauty that makes a good filler between perennials is borage. Grown inland, this herb tends to get gangly, but here at the coast, it has a bushy habit.

An herb virtue certainly worth mentioning is that deer don't seem to care much for them. You may see signs of a nibble here and there, but that will be the extent of their taste test. There are too many herbs to highlight here, but I do want to feature those that grow well by the sea that I cannot do without, and

Johnny jump ups can grow just about anywhere—even among beach stones.

Seaside Suggestion

Do something out of the blue with borage blooms. The tiny star-shaped, sky-blue flowers of this plant make an interesting garnish, as there are no truly blue foods. ("Blue" cabbage is rather red-purple in colour, and blueberries lean more toward blue-black.) Sprinkle electric-blue borage blossoms over salads, fruit platters, or floating over a bowl of punch. For a touch of seaside herb novelty, float them over wine or spirits.

Borage blooms over a fine red wine

Freshly picked, flavourful, fragrant culinary herbs from my coastal garden

what I do with them. I have classed them in the most commonly used catagories: culinary, garnish, aromatic, ornamental, and medicinal.

CULINARY HERBS

Culinary herbs are plants that enhance the flavours and aromas of food and drinks. It doesn't take much. One need only add a few snippets of this and that herb over a dish to tingle the senses. Using herbs with food can also reduce cravings for fatty sauces, butter, and salt, with the added benefit of introducing additional vitamins and minerals to your diet, particularly when fresh herbs are used. The most commonly used culinary herbs are mentioned in "Surf-and-Herb Recipes" (see p. 162)

Arugula cannot go unmentioned because it grows extremely well at the coast. On my property, some plants have even self-seeded at the water's edge. This plant may be considered a salad green by some, but since it's warm, bitter, buttery flavour is so intense, it is best used as an accent in salads and sandwiches. In that case it is an herb.

Easy-to-grow arugula is a popular addition to mixed salad greens.

An additional virtue of culinary herbs is that they can spare parents nagging, "Eat your vegetables!" Visiting friends whose children are very fussy eaters are surprised when there are no vegetables left on the lunch plate I prepare for them. Just a little pinch of fresh oregano or finely chopped basil and a dribble of honey make "boring" steamed veggies look, smell, and taste interesting. Herbs not only enhance the flavour and aroma of foods, but they also embellish the presentation of any dish. A little kitchen garden is a culinary herb garden. If space is an issue, grow herbs in containers, and move them to a sheltered spot on stormy days.

HERBS AS GARNISH

Garnishes add colour and texture to improve the presentation and appearance of a dish. Picture the difference between a plain block of cheese on a plate, and a block of cheese surrounded by a medley of aromatic herbs, like lacey dill leaves, blades of chives, or freshly picked basil. Spectacular! As soon as nasturtiums come into bloom, I find a place for them at the table: as a bouquet of appetite-stimulating colours, as

Container herbs by the sea

Herbs in any combination enhance the presentation and aroma of foods.

garnish on a plate, and sometimes even in a salad to add a bit of peppery zip. Herbs are visually pleasing, even if they are sitting fresh in a jar of water waiting to be used, or hanging to dry for future use.

Parsley is probably the most popular herb garnish. The restaurant industry in North America spends millions on it, only to see much of it thrown out. This is a shame, since raw parsley has the highest nutritional value of all herbs and can be consumed with just about any food when minced finely. It has

A tea lover's hanging chamomile plants

COASTAL TIP

Parsley is usually an annual in the Maritimes, but at the coast, where winter temperatures are milder, it behaves more like a perennial. Each year the plant gets larger and produces more seed heads, but the leaves remain just as fresh and flavourful. If growing parsley in a container, sink it to ground level near the compost pile to overwinter with a few bows of spruce on top for extra protection from extreme temperature fluctuations. Don't cut it back. It will be there for you to pick all through the winter. The following spring, as the days get longer, parsley will begin to put out new growth for the next season.

a subtle "grassy" taste that enhances other flavours and blends in well with other herbs. Keeping freshly picked parsley placed in water on the windowsill inspires creativity in the kitchen. It reminds me of the vast herb possibilities while preparing a meal.

AROMATIC HERBS

Aromatic herbs are best noticed and appreciated along a pathway, as a border, or in a sitting area. All herbs are aromatic. Some are grown specifically for adding aroma and flavour to food while others are best suited for fresh and simple olfactory pleasures. Having aromatic herbs growing at arm's length invites picking a leaf or two and bringing them up close to your nose. For a moment, you will be lost in thoughts about the wonders of nature, and perhaps a few sweet personal memories. This is aromatherapy: a fragrant experience that is both exhilarating and evasive. Like a kite on a thin string, the scent fades away high into the

Desipte its delicate appearance, lavender thrives at the coast. Seaside lavender has a slightly minty fragrance.

Mint grown between two decks

sky, as fresh, bruised leaves express their best aroma in the first ten minutes. Never hesitate having this brief, engaging scratch-and-sniff experience during a stroll through the garden. Herbs are very forgiving of being picked.

A wonderful, carefree, fragrant herb deserving of being set apart from the rest is lavender. Planted on an "island" on its own, it becomes a focal point of the seaside garden.

Mints grow extremely well at the coast. They can quickly take over, but will behave themselves in isolated corners, like these adjoining seaside decks. There it will stay out of mischief—it has nowhere else to go but up. When cornered, it is both easily accessible and attractive. Mint is immensely enjoyed as a therapeutic aromatic herb. Take a few seconds to pick a leaf whenever you are near it, crush it, and inhale. These days, mint comes in many varieties of scents: chocolate, spearmint, apple, peppermint, pineapple, and more. Infused, fresh or dried, mint makes a soothing caffeine-free tea. Finely chopped, it makes a refreshing addition to cold drinks and desserts. Try it over fruit salad, cheesecake, custard, and pies. (For my favourite garden-fresh recipe, see p. 124.)

Annual geraniums are superbly fragrant. The showiest have a strong carrot scent. These cultivars have been developed for their large coin-sized blooms that range from reds to pinks to whites. The most amazing are two-toned in colour. The commonly named "scented geraniums" are a scented-leaf pelargonium with much smaller, rather insignificant, flowers. They are, however, increasing in popularity for their scented foliage, which can smell of lemon, rose, apple, cinnamon, orange, peach, even chocolate. Cranesbill, a perennial geranium, is an exception to this rule. It has long-lasting brilliant fuchsia pink blooms with foliage that, according to the wives of fishers, smell like "a rich man's aftershave." This perennial blooms profusely for over three weeks and makes a great dense ground cover.

Seaside Suggestion

Clip flowering lavender shoots just before maturity when they are still closed and firm. Tie them together at the base with an elastic band. Place lavender bouquets in with towels or the linen closet to add a sweet, fresh scent to sheets. A few lavender sprigs tied with a ribbon on a pillow are sure to leave lifelong memories of seaside comfort for those who stay overnight.

Dried lavender sprigs

ORNAMENTAL HERBS

Most ornamental herbs had their start as a remedy for some ailment, but few of us grow herbs for medicinal or therapeutic uses these days. The same can be said of herbal teas. Beebalm (or bergamot) for example, is used in Earl Grey tea, but we would not, as a rule, grow it for that use. We grow beebalm simply for its attractive floral display. And it thrives at the coast!

There are a number of popular "ornamental herbs" that at one time were grown principally not so much for their aesthetic appeal, but for their medicinal use. Some are still in use today (see "Medicinal Herbs," p. 159). But I think it is safe to say though that the roles of many "medicinal" herbs dating from the peak of alchemy in Medieval Europe (1200–1500) have been either forgotten or rendered dubious. Lady's mantel is one of those speculative stories. Planted by the sea, lady's mantel is admired for its endurance of the elements. It is particularly showy when in bloom: its wispy clouds of cheery, minuscule chartreuse flowers go well with any plant combination. This plant

Lady's mantel makes a lovely border while also suppressing weeds.

Nasturtium blooms against the palette of the sea make a striking display.

Creeping thyme spills out beautifully onto surfaces where nothing else can grow.

was originally called "Our Lady's Mantel." Mystics perceived the scalloped leaves of this plant to be the Virgin Mary's cloak, and thus believed it had properties able to cure "women's problems."

Nasturtium is commonly listed as an herb because of its edible flowers. While nasturtium is a beautiful plant in the garden and as a garnish, its pungent peppery flavour is overpowering and bitter to most, and is an acquired taste (see p. 51 on how to grow it from seed).

I think all herbs are attractive wherever they are grown, but thyme is also one of the most diverse. Together, culinary thymes, fragrant thymes, and ground cover thymes amount to as many as thirty varieties. In rockeries they can roam freely without getting into trouble with other plants. Thyme, left to spill over a boulder or onto a walkway to hug the ground, is a gem, especially when in bloom. Although fragrant and flavourful, this herb is often grown simply because it blooms profusely and makes a great ground cover. Blooms come in several shades of pink and last only about a week, but are well worth it for the display. Thyme is often used to fill in tiny, defined spaces between stepping stones or brick walkways. It is easily trimmed back from solid surfaces. There are several varieties available these days, but woolly thyme sports leaves that are fuzzy and minty-green—a most appropriate colour for the seaside setting. Fragrance and flavour can range from peppery to clove-like to citrusy, depending on the variety. Thyme is named for its fragrant attributes: lemon thyme, coconut thyme, lavender thyme, mint thyme, oregano thyme, and so on.

MEDICINAL HERBS

Medicinal herbs are plants that have been experimented with since our hunter-gatherer ancestors, when they were used as poultices for the relief of insect bites and flesh wounds. In the Middle Ages, using herbs to heal various ailments fell under what

Echinacea is an attractive, rose-red, daisy-like flower whose essence is known to ward off colds. It can be started indoors from seed and grows extremely well by the sea. As with most perennials, it blooms the following year.

was considered "alchemy." These were hit-and-miss experiments. However, we can be grateful for the plant properties discovered back then for many of the modern pharmaceuticals and holistic medicines used successfully today. Echinacea, as an example, has been effective in reducing the severity and duration of common cold symptoms. Cloves aid in reducing inflammation and toothaches. Witch hazel is used as a natural astringent to reduce scarring and bruises. Chamomile tea acts as a muscle relaxant.

Researchers are always discovering promising new plant-based compounds. As an example, a common

Cannabis is reputed to have many healing properties. Its nickname, "weed," must refer to the fact that it grows as prolifically as one—even by the sea!

little garden ornamental called rosy periwinkle is the source for a drug called Vinblastine for treating Hodgkins' disease, and another called Vincristine, used in treatment for leukemia. Let's not forget the powerful painkiller morphine, derived from the opium poppy. The list of beneficial medicinal plants goes on and on.

On the home front, the use of "medicinal herbs" should be limited to aromatherapy and well-known plants for preparing soothing teas and tonics, or herb-infused baths to relieve stress. Leave the rest to the experts: visit a doctor or a health and wellness centre for safe medicinal herb products.

I was surprised to come across the most notorious of medicinal herbs growing so vigorously by the sea. This explained why this particular seaside gardener was so reluctant to speak to me. Most have been flattered by my interest to take pictures of their seaside garden for the book. The herb in question is cannabis, also called medical marijuana. Cannabis, despite its healing and anti-inflammatory properties, is still illegal to grow, possess, and use in Canada. One must be granted a medical marijuana permit.

PRESERVING HERBS YEAR-ROUND

The trouble with trying to grow herbs indoors in a northern coastal climate is that that we have four seasons. The days get too short during winter months.

Even when I chase the sunspots around the house, our latitude at that time of year offers insufficient sunlight to sustain proper photosynthesis. While grow lights can give herbs a good start, they are not beneficial for extended periods. Indoor winter herbs will eventually result in tasteless pale, weak, spindly plants. A far superior way to enjoy herbs over the winter months is to pick them at their peak from the great outdoors, during the summer, and either dry them, use them to make savoury vinegars, or freeze them.

FREEZING HERBS

All leaf-based herbs freeze well, except for basil (it turns black). All you have to do is immerse your chosen herbs in any liquid—plain water, butter, gravy, prepared broths, cream of chicken, slightly diluted honey or maple syrup so that it solidifies just below the freezing mark. Give your freshly picked herbs a good shake to rid them of possible debris or insects by whipping them over a clean, hard surface like a countertop. This also releases the aromatic and flavourful oils of your herbs. Chop finely the useful parts of the plant and spread them equally throughout an ice cube tray for perfect portion sizes. Then pour your liquid base of choice over them. Be sure to label your herbs, they all look alike once frozen in liquid. This is a great way to have your favourite herb combinations ready to go on any given day of the year.

Ice cube trays provide perfectly preserved herb portions.

DRYING CULINARY HERBS

Herbs dry exceptionally well. Although flavours do change somewhat once dried, their signature character remains. To dry culinary herb plants, tie them at their base and hang upside down in a reasonably dry location away from direct sunlight. Some dedicated gardeners choose to invest in a dehydration kit because it is quick and is a good space saver. There is no need to have plants hung to dry all over the house. Bear in mind that once moisture has been extracted, an herb's flavour becomes more concentrated. Keep thoroughly dried herbs in airtight containers at room temperature, again away from direct sunlight. I keep mine stored in baby food bottles in a kitchen drawer. This is a convenient way to bring a bit of summer flare into winter dishes and teas.

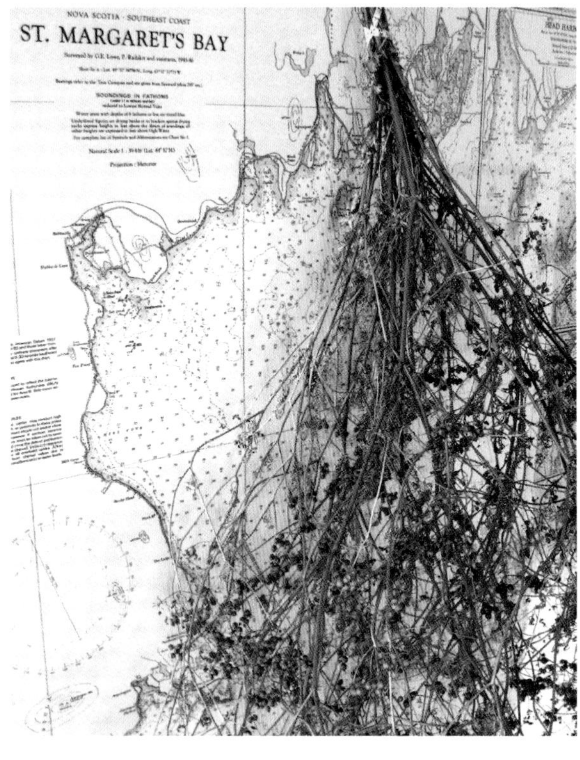

Coriander seeds of the cilantro plant are hung indoors to dry and cure for winter storage.

SAVOURY HERB VINEGARS AND PICKLES

A natural preservative with a long shelf life is vinegar. It will keep just about anything suspended in time and will take on the character of the herb it contains. Herbs, coincidentally, add aromatic and flavourful dimensions to vinegar. I am partial to cider vinegars and encourage experimenting with various types, except red wine vinegars (balsamic), as they tend to discolour herbal infusions.

Here's how to preserve herbs in vinegar: Simply rinse and pat dry your favourite herb combinations. Allow them to sit at room temperature for a couple of hours for excess water to evaporate. This way the vinegar won't get watered down when you introduce them to it. Ratio is not an issue. Cloves and garlic are always pleasant additions. Homemade savoury herb vinegars also make excellent pickling agents.

Pickling is a popular easy way to use culinary herbs. One of my favourite garden goodies to pickle is bush bean. I always end up with more than we can eat and freeze at harvest time, so I also pickle them. They are great as a condiment. Place one or two beans in a spicy drink like Bloody Mary for a novelty conversation starter. They are also quite nice served as a side when drained and boiled in fresh water.

Pickled yellow bush beans

SURF-AND-HERB RECIPES

If you love seafood, grow herbs. If you don't know what to do with herbs, use them with seafood. It's that simple. Herbs give seafood an infusion of wholesome natural flavours and aromas, and seafood is the crown to which my favourite herbs get a chance to shine as jewels to wow the senses! Here are a few spectacular herb-seafood pairings that require the simplest of ingredients and are quick to prepare. When it comes to using herbs in cooking, there are no set rules for quantity. If subtle flavour is what you are after, use less. If a particular herb really excites your palate, be bold and use more of it.

Fresh lovage leaves and chives over lobster is most aromatic.

Seaside lovage

LOVAGE

LOVAGE-STUFFED MACKEREL

Serves 2

For those who are not familiar with lovage, it is a perennial herb grown for its celery-like flavoured leaves. Lovage leaves can be used in any dish where celery would be called for: soups, stews, poultry dressings, casseroles, chowder, wraps, salads, etc. The main reason I like to grow lovage is because it is fresh for the picking all season long, as it grows from May until the first frost, and makes a handsome yellow-green tender shrub. During the "mackerel run" it has become a tradition at my house to have fresh lovage-stuffed mackerel done on the barbeque to celebrate the arrival of summer. This usually takes place early to mid-June.

Lovage-stuffed Mackerel

- 2 medium-sized mackerel
- 4–5 sprigs lovage (per mackerel)
- 2–3 lemon slices (per mackerel)

1. Clean the fish as usual, and then place a generous amount of lovage leaves in the body cavity. Place a few slices of lemon on top.

2. Wrap the stuffed fish in tinfoil and cook on the barbeque, lid down, 10–15 minutes. The natural, healthy fish oils take up the savoury herbal filling.

Serve with new steamed potatoes and a little salad.

CORIANDER

CORIANDER MAPLE SALMON

Serves 4

Coriander is among the easiest herbs to grow by the sea. It has two types of leaves. The lower, less lacey leaves called "cilantro" are preferable for culinary use. They have a unique, warm, citrus-like flavour and aroma. The seeds, called coriander, are usually collected when mature and tan in colour. These hard seeds are mostly used in pickling or crushed for use in spice blends. But when still green, coriander has a gentle crunch with a mild, nutty-citrus flavour and a lingering warm aftertaste.

- 1 large salmon half, filleted, skin on
- 125 ml (1/2 cup) pure maple syrup (per fillet)
- fresh green coriander seeds (about 1/2 handful)
- 5 ml (1 tsp) cracked pepper

Coriander Maple Salmon

1. Place salmon fillet, skin down, on rimmed baking sheet (reserved for barbeque only). Using a sharp knife, score the fillet vertically all the way to the tail about every 2 cm (1/4 in.). Pour maple syrup over fish fillet and into the cuts. Sprinkle generously with green coriander seeds and a bit of cracked pepper.

2. Place the baking sheet with salmon on the barbeque, lid down, for about 15 minutes until salmon sides sizzle and centre of fish is opaque.

Serve with steamed rice topped with asparagus (cooked al dente) and a bit of butter.

Young green coriander seeds

Serving of Dill Sole Rolls

Dill

DILL

DILL SOLE ROLLS

Serves 2 (as a side)

Fresh dill is an invaluable plant in the kitchen. Its delicate, lacey leaves are as flavourful as they are graceful. Grow it away from strong winds; it is a tall plant that can easily bend and break off. Both dill leaves and seeds are used in cooking. An easy self-seeder, it will return on its own throughout the vegetable garden, year after year.

- 1 medium zucchini
- 45 ml (3 tbsp) garlic butter
- 6–8 sole fillets, bone out
- 125 ml (1/2 cup) prepared cream of chicken soup
- 75 ml (1/3 cup) chopped fresh dill

1. Cut zucchini into sticks the width of sole fillets. In a pan, sauté sticks in garlic butter and dill leaves for 3 minutes.

2. Place zucchini sticks at one end of the fillets and roll it up. Place sole rolls in a baking dish. Sprinkle with more dill (and optional green coriander seeds) and pour prepared cream of chicken soup over the rolls, just covering the bottom of the pan. Bake at 350° F (180° C) for 20 minutes.

Serve over garden-fresh beet leaves and/or with steamed baby potatoes.

OREGANO

OREGANO PAN-FRIED HADDOCK

Serves 2–4 (depending on size of fillets)

Oregano is popular in Italian cuisine but should not be limited to pizza and pasta dishes. Its robust, sharp taste blends extremely well with the delicate flavour of haddock and other white fish. In addition to its easy-to-prepare, crunchy finish, oregano gives haddock a wonderful and unique herbal lift.

- 125 ml (1/2 cup) Corn Flakes crumbs (crush with a rolling pin)
- 30 ml (2 tbsp) Southern Style Chicken Shake 'N Bake
- 60 ml (1/4 cup) fresh oregano leaves (chop if larger than confetti)
- canola oil
- 2–3 fresh haddock fillets

1. In a large mixing bowl, combine crushed Corn Flakes crumbs and Southern Style Chicken Shake 'N Bake. Whip sprigs of oregano against the counter a few times to release fragrance. Pick leaves from stems and mix into dry ingredient mixture.

Oregano Pan-Fried Haddock

2. Drizzle oil on bottom of non-stick skillet. Preheat. When a drop of water in the skillet bounces around and evaporates immediately, it is ready for the fish.

3. Pat fish dry with paper towel and cover with the mixture. Cook just a couple of minutes, turning fillets over twice, until interior is opaque and juicy.

Serve with mashed potatoes and coleslaw.

Oregano

Lemon grass

Lemon balm

LEMON HERBS

STEAMED LEMON-HERB CLAMS

Serves 2

We may not be able to grow our own lemons here at the coast, but we can certainly grow lemon balm, lemon grass, and lemon-scented geranium (use indoor-grown lemon-scented geranium during winter months). These easy herbs are a seaside cook's best-kept secret. Lemon balm, like mint, is especially hardy in the Maritimes. It can be grown right at water's edge. These lemon-flavoured/-scented herbs can be used wherever lemon would be called for, but are much milder. As with lemon, the leaves of these herbs are used to add flavour and aroma, but they are not necessarily eaten. Serving them left in is optional, but added fresh as a garnish is a *must* that will add a touch of aromatic class to this mildly lemon-infused shellfish. You can also use steamed oysters, mussels, or quahogs.

- 20 medium-sized fresh clams
- 125 ml (1/2 cup) lemon-flavoured herb or a blend of lemon balm, scented geranium, and lemon grass
- 15 ml (1 tbsp) prepared garlic butter

Garnish

- fresh lemon herb leaves; sprinkle chopped chives

1. Give fresh clams a good rinse to remove potential sand particles. In a large pot, boil enough water to cover clams. Drop clams into pot with several sprigs of your choice of lemon-flavoured/-scented herb.

2. When clamshells have all opened, about 10 minutes, turn heat off and allow to "rest," lid on, for another 5 minutes. Remove clams using tongs.

3. Reserve about 375 ml (1 1/2 cups) of the broth and add garlic butter to taste for dipping the clams.

4. Serve clams with your choice of freshly picked lemon herb leaves and a sprinkle of chopped chives.

Serving tip: Clams are best served in their own bowl or plate as sand may come in contact with other foods. Begin with a hardy salad of your choice, followed by clams on their own.

Steamed Lemon-Herb Clams with lemon balm leaves

CHIVES

BBQ CHIVE-COATED SEA TROUT

Serves 2–4 (depending on size of fillet)

Chives are the most versatile and indispensable of kitchen herbs. This plant, which puts out a long-lasting display of lovely lavender-coloured flowers, can be grown anywhere on a coastal property and will grow back as soon as it is cut. The blades are tender and hollow, and chopping them releases the goodness. Its mild, sweet onion flavour and aroma combines well with every other herb and spice.

BBQ Chive-coated Sea Trout

* 1 sea trout fillet, skin on
* 2.5 ml (1/2 tsp) celery salt
* 60 ml (1/4 cup) chopped fresh chives

1. Place trout fillet skin down on a sheet of extra-strength tinfoil and fold the sides up to about 3 cm (1 in.) from the fish.

2. Sprinkle a bit of celery salt, then cover the fish in chopped fresh chives.

3. Barbeque sea trout, lid down, for about 10 minutes until sides sizzle and centre of fish is opaque.

Serve with a side dish of steamed basmati rice with drizzle of olive oil and fresh mini tomatoes.

Fresh chives

BASIL

BASIL AND BRIE SHRIMP PASTA

Serves 2

Basil is a warm-climate herb that will thrive in the seaside garden when given good fertile soil and protection from harsh winds. It has a distinct cinnamon-like flavour and works very well with cheeses and pasta dishes. Since basil does not like cold, never store it in the refrigerator but in a glass of water at room temperature, preferably on a bright windowsill. Treated well, it can last almost a week this way.

Basil and Brie Shrimp Pasta

- 16–20 medium shrimp, cooked, shells removed
- 1 cup basil leaves, chopped
- 2 medium tomatoes, diced
- 1 medium-sized wedge or small package Brie, cubed (about 1 cm [1/4 in.] each)
- 15 ml (1 tbsp) olive oil
- 100 g (4 oz.) Capelli Dangelo pasta
- 125 ml (1/2 cup) pine nuts (optional)
- salt and pepper to taste

1. Toss together chopped basil, diced tomatoes, and Brie wedges in a bowl with cooked, peeled shrimp (if shrimp are frozen, allow them to reach room temperature).

2. Bring to a boil Capelli Dangelo pasta (spaghettini will do) for two, until al-dente.

3. Drain pasta and add to ingredients. Mix well.

4. Microwave 2 minutes just before serving with salt and pepper to taste, and optional pine nuts.

Fresh basil leaves

PARSLEY

GOLDEN GARLIC AND PARSLEY SCALLOPS

Serves 2

Parsley has the uncanny ability to enhance natural flavours. Paired with garlic on seafood, it is heavenly. The magic of garlic in cooking cannot be underestimated, and the aroma of it in the kitchen stimulates the appetite. It is best grown from little bulbs, like those used for growing onion sets. As with onion, garlic is taken up to dry in late fall for use throughout the winter. Another way to stretch the life of garlic is to make garlic butter and freeze it in ice cube trays for quick future use: simply boil garlic cloves until soft, crush them into butter at room temperature, then freeze in an ice cube tray for quick individual portions.

- 1 ml (1/4 tsp) sea salt
- 2 cloves fresh garlic, grated
- 75 ml (1/4 cup) finely chopped fresh parsley
- 30 ml (2 tbsp) olive oil
- 40 small (or 20 large) scallops
- 75 ml (1/4 cup) dry white wine (optional)*

1. Crush sea salt into grated garlic with a fork. Place mixture in a glass bowl, and add minced parsley and olive oil. Mix well.

Golden Garlic and Parsley Scallops

2. Pat dry fresh scallops with paper towel and add them to glass bowl mixture. Toss well, then cover the bowl in plastic and allow flavours to blend as they sit at room temperature, about 20–30 minutes.

3. Remove mixture and place in very hot non-stick pan. Sear for about 5 minutes or until scrallops are opaque in the centre. Be careful not to overcook. Remove from heat as soon as they appear to "sweat."

*Optional: pour dry white wine over the cooked scallops just before removing them from the pan.

Serve immediately over your choice of plain rice or pasta.

Moss curled variety of parsley

SUMMER SAVORY

SUMMER SAVORY FISH CAKES

Serves 4

Summer savory is an annual that grows surprisingly well at the coast. Just one plant goes a long way. Use it fresh or dry, but in moderation. It is quite spicy, and just a hint of it in these fish cakes adds a bit of colour and mouthwatering flavour.

- 1 small onion, chopped
- 5 ml (1 tsp) butter
- 4 medium potatoes, peeled
- 3–4 fillets fresh haddock
- 5 ml (1 tsp) minced dry or fresh summer savory
- 60 ml (1/4 cup) all-purpose flour
- 15 ml (1 tbsp) canola oil

1. Sauté onion in butter until translucent (do not allow to caramelize) using the pot that potatoes will be boiled in. Remove onion and set aside. Place potatoes in the pot (do not wash it out) and cover them with water. Bring to a boil. Meanwhile, cube the fish fillets with scissors.

2. When potatoes are soft, add the fish in with them. Turn heat off and keep pot covered about 5 minutes. The haddock will cook but not fall apart.

3. Drain the water from pot. Add summer savory and return sautéed onion. Mash ingredients together. Cover the pot and allow flavours to blend.

4. When the mixture has cooled enough to handle, form it into burger-sized patties. Sprinkle with a bit of flour. Fry in a non-stick pan with a bit of canola oil until golden.

Serve with a light salad, fresh garden spinach greens or with a side of steamed garden vegetables like broccoli, bush beans, peas, or baby carrots.

Summer savory

Summer Savory Fish Cakes

Herb Medley Seafood Chowder

HERB MEDLEY

HERB MEDLEY SEAFOOD CHOWDER

Serves 4

Enjoy this lovely, easy-to-prepare chowder, which combines a few mild herbs during the cooking process to give it a flavourful base, while a favourite, more "distinct" herb is added as the main accent. Later, use whichever herbs you happen to have in the garden, and lots of what you like best. There are no set rules. Go with your palate. Any seafood will do as long as there are no bones, skin, or shells: solo or combined, use any combination of filleted white fish, salmon, shrimp, lobster, crab, or small scallops.

Chowder

* 3 celery stalks, chopped
* 1 onion, finely chopped
* 15 ml (1 tbsp) butter
* 4 medium potatoes, peeled and cubed
* 1 cube Knorr chicken bouillon
* (1/2 cup) chopped mild herbs (chives, parsley, orache, and lovage work well together)
* 2 cups raw seafood
* 1 (170 ml [3/4 cup]) can Carnation thick cream, or 250 ml (1 cup) fresh cream

Garnish

* One of these distinctly flavoured herbs: lovage, summer savory, thyme, oregano, dill, or cilantro

Garnish collection on kitchen window

1. In a large pot, sauté celery and onion in butter until translucent. Do not allow these to caramelize.

2. Add potatoes with just enough water to cover them with Knorr bouillon cube. Simmer until potatoes have softened, between 5–10 minutes (be careful not to overcook them).

3. Add mild herbs with raw seafood and heat until fish is opaque. If using cooked lobster and/or cooked shrimp, add when all other ingredients are thoroughly cooked.

4. Stir in cream. Heat, but do not boil.

Serve each bowl with a sprinkle of one of the distinctly flavoured herbs listed.

Bon appétit by the sea!

11

Let the Sea Steal the Show

Never work harder than you have to;
live as gloriously as you can.
—Merilyn Simonds—

Are you the type of gardener who thinks: *I should have spent more of my free time watering the garden, mowing and raking the lawn, digging out dandelions, edging the driveway and paths, painting the fence, clipping the hedge, applying fertilizers, weeding and deadheading the flowers?* I can honestly say that I have learned to do away with those ominous to-do lists. Certain styles of gardening are far too demanding, especially in the challenging setting of the sea. Since moving to the coast, I have adopted a mental *to-be* list. I take time to look and see, touch, and feel the living ocean. Above all, I have learned to be silent and listen. (How interesting...these two words share the same letters.)

Through these experiences, I have learned that the only way to grow a garden that evokes, for me, a sense of well-being and relaxation is to surround myself with plants that grow effortlessly by the sea. Forget about growing nostalgic plants like peony, delphinium, magnolia, and lilac in the path of oceanic extremes. Some plants do not belong at the coast and will be happier and healthier in stable inland conditions. Many ornamentals struggle here. Weeping varieties, fancy grafted conifers, and topiaries eventually succumb to a slow, agonizing death. Coastal life is torture for some plants, and will cause the conscientious gardener undue stress.

One plant I have been obsessed with is corkscrew hazel (zone 5). When I first discovered it growing at the base of an old Victorian lamppost at the entrance of a farmhouse in the valley of Nova Scotia (which is far removed from the sea), it was love at first sight. When we finally got moved into our present seaside home, I was given three of them as a housewarming gift—a very thoughtful gesture by a fellow artist who knew about my fetish for spirals and my insistence on grouping rather than planting one of everything. (I use the spiral motif often in my artwork. It evokes for me the cycles of life, longevity, and hope.) These three plants glowed of health and hardiness. But no more than a week into the ground, they began to scream, *Get us out of here!* I lived in mortal fear of being charged with plant cruelty by the SPCA, who would ban me from possessing garden plants for life. The hazel's progressive shredding foliage and breaking limbs stressed me out terribly. I couldn't stand to see them suffer.

Although I had planted the corkscrew hazel in fertile soil in a protected area of the yard, they still didn't make it. The salty air, wind, and fog (and the fact that they are hardy only to zone 5) completely did them in. It was a major setback. Many

Carefree daisies dance in the sea breeze

well-intentioned gardeners give up in the face of such disasters. Occasionally, as with life in general, there are some disappointments. But, hey! Do we not learn more from our failures than from our successes? It is so important to choose plants well for the coastal garden. I have also learned that simplicity over complexity is best. These days, I think of my coastal gardens as little condiments and garnishes that enhance the experience of the main course: the sea. Keeping the seaside garden simple and manageable is important to the overall enjoyment of a coastal property. The view takes care of the rest. Let the sea steal the show.

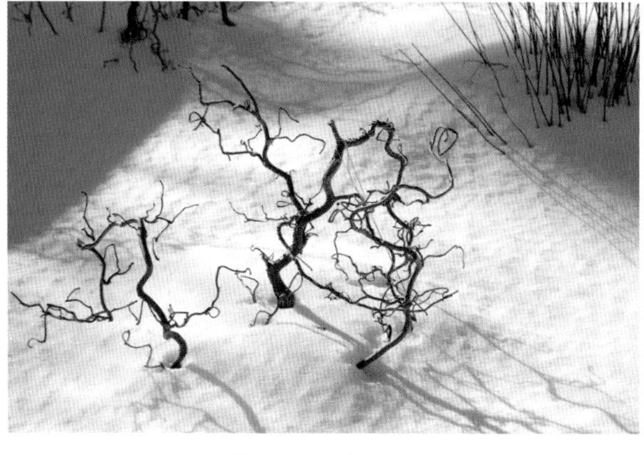

Last show for corkscrew hazels

GARDENS THAT COMPLEMENT, NOT COMPETE

Oceanfront homeowners may forget the sea's power to seduce the onlooker. Having a view of the water, no matter how marginal, infers a sense of awe all of its own. Seaside gardening is unique in that it takes place in a setting that already commands attention. Whether your oceanfront overlooks a tranquil estuary, a cove, a little beach, or the bold, open Atlantic,

A simple setting that commands attention

Sweet and simple seaside garden

the water will be the first thing to draw attention. People have an innate sense that the ocean is much bigger and deeper than the sum of its visible parts. By this, I mean that you do not need to grow big, glamorous gardens—that is a look more appropriate for the royals and for formal, public gardens. There is no need to put yourself through all that trouble, time, and expense only to end up with difficult-to-maintain extravagance that will distract from the majesty of the sea. A coastal garden should *complement* rather than *compete* with the view of water.

When coastal gardens appear as natural as the surrounding scenery, it seems like they have always been there. Ideally, you want plants that are low-care—plants that can take care of themselves. Native vegetation certainly meets that criterion. Gardening should be pleasurable and create a place of repose. If yours is frustrating and takes up so much time that you're left with little energy to enjoy life by the sea with family and friends, adjustments are needed. Some homeowners may have the luxury of hiring a landscaping company to keep elaborate gardens looking good. But for most of us, the cost can easily become prohibitive and that becomes a stress in itself. This is not gardening for pleasure. An assessment of your approach to seaside gardening will help refocus your priorities. A different mindset of how a garden by the sea *should* look can make all the difference in the world.

When I attended the Nova Scotia College of Art and Design University, I heard, on occasion, that the the more time you spend there worse an artist you can become. We can so easily lose perspective. The point here is that sometimes we gardening enthusiasts surround ourselves with too many gardening books. I am certainly guilty. Those images of flawless flowers in perfectly arranged stills can cause a seaside gardener to chase unrealistic goals. My father often poked fun at my collection of books and magazines on gardening. He would say: "All you need to know are two things. One: dig a hole. Two: Plant it green-side up." His message: Fancy by the sea results in failure. My dad, *jardinier extraordinaire*, could see that I was setting myself up for failure with exotic inland garden fantasies. Yes, I learned the hard way. I was indeed chasing after a certain look that could not be achieved at the coast.

Once again, remember that the view of water will detract attention from your perceived neglect or poor gardening skills. Choose your battles and take them in stride. I am not overly protective of my plants; they must fend for themselves. I have resigned to leaving it to the survival of the fittest. If erecting a protective tent around a specimen is the only way to ensure it survives our coastal winters...well, it is out of luck in my garden. These contraptions get blown away in no time where I live. This is another reason why I am careful to choose plants with coastal characteristics (see p. 23). If your seaside garden is more frustrating than gratifying, you probably are trying too hard to achieve a certain look. Whichever gardening style you prefer, be aware of the fact that you may not always have the control that you would like by the sea. As mentioned before, to avoid winterkill, leaf windburn, blasted-off petals, and broken branches opening the door to disease, choose your plants well from the start and keep it simple.

It is a different world out here. At the coast, we have to work with what the environment throws at us. If we try to work against it, seaside gardening becomes a chore rather than a pleasure, and discouraging rather than gratifying. The point of seaside

Lupins are an excellent flower for the coast. They take care of themselves and return faithfully each summer.

gardening is to create outdoor spaces where one can take deep breaths of fresh, fragrant, salty air and feel at one with the universe. It should not be an enormous amount of work and anxiety, but rather a pleasant activity that keeps us connected with the cycles of life. Some maintenance is always required. When it is necessary to get on your hands and knees, think of it as "kneeling" and your seaside garden will become a little work of *heart*. Don't feel so pressured to have tons of colour at all times. Work around what is already growing; look for little natural surprises and allow for more greens of various tones, heights, and textures to foster a lush, restful atmosphere. It *is* easy being green, here.

SPIRALS AND THE SEA

I am once again reminded of the spiral. I have often asked myself why I am so attracted to this shape. I suppose it is a metaphor for how life forms seem to unravel so simply and elegantly, despite all of their unseen complexities. We humans tend to like pure geometrical shapes. They are easy to remember and to draw. They allow us the illusion of having control over how the world works. Simple shapes anchor us and give us a sense of comprehension, when in reality life on Earth is a soup of chance events.... Our attempts to achieve order are at best managed chaos, like the sea.

It is amazing how common the spiral motif is in the ocean. Think of it. Waves alone are ongoing undulating spirals. Seashells come in a variety of spiral shapes. Many creatures of the sea sport spiral-like bodies—the tail of a seahorse for instance. Long-armed starfish appear to mimic the shape of spinning galaxies. Our DNA, the double helix of the human genome, is essentially spiral in its configuration.

Back down to Earth, let's ponder how mariners coil their ropes into spirals. Spiders' webs are spiral-based. Clinging vines have spiralling tendrils to help find their way up toward the sun. Young, spiral-shaped ferns are one of the first plants to pierce through the cool spring soil. Gradually, they open into loose, wispy arms that sway in the ocean breeze just as elegantly as sea plants dancing in their watery world.

A native fern is always welcomed in the seaside setting. Ferns demand nothing of me except my

A moonshell, spiral of the sea

Coastal Tip

Ready-for-harvest fiddleheads tell us that there will be no more frost. It is now safe to plant your seaside vegetable garden.

Ready-to-savour fiddleheads

admiring gaze. But the most exciting part of spring for me, as an Acadian, is when fiddleheads (young ostrich ferns) that grow along the banks of freshwater rivers are ready for picking. This succulent native plant heralds the onset of summer. Boil fiddleheads in sea water and serve them with a dollop of butter. They are so good and wholesome prepared this way.

A casual, low-maintenance embankment of perennials

THE CASUAL, CAREFREE COASTAL GARDEN

As mentioned earlier, to achieve a certain coastal atmosphere that stirs the soul, think simplicity over complexity. Aim for a naturalistic style of gardening. Look to the coast itself for inspiration. Tall grasses, densely clustered shrubs, silvery foliage, dwarf specimens, and low-growing plants abound. Having an informal approach to gardening will help you achieve that unique, beachy, coastal style (see chapter 2).

The term "naturalistic" means that which imitates nature closely. In its purest sense, a natural yard would mean returning the land to its pre-colonial state. That is far too extreme an approach. A naturalistic yard looks as though it has grown from naturally dispersed seed rather than from carefully

Gabrielle taking time out by the sea in style

placed nursery stock. A casual, carefree garden has a free spirit. It is an unpretentious element of the seaside setting. It does not draw attention away from the sea. It stands on its own as a part of the easygoing lifestyle associated with coastal living. Now and then, in stages and phases, flowering plants take turns in delighting us with their little splashes of colour.

A BIT OF SEASIDE *LAISSEZ-FAIRE*

The French term *laissez-faire* essentially means, "let it be." In the context of seaside gardening, having a *laissez-faire* attitude means not being a garden workaholic. Learn to let go and enjoy the coastal garden as it is and put aside its perceived flaws. Keeping the garden manageable is possible without taking up lots of your free time (see chapter 5).

A few native plants moving in among your cultivated gardens should be no reason for alarm. Buttercup flowers are to me, a welcome spark of cheery yellow amidst favourite perennials. I do, however, snip off spent blooms to prevent excessive amounts of seed from setting up camp. I also keep its creeping roots in check only once a year: in early spring.

Clumps of native tall grasses, like bulrush, marram grass, and American dune grass, add a graceful touch to the coastal garden. As long as native and

Perennial shasta daisies and bachelor buttons need no attention; weathered lawn chairs need no touch-ups. Relax guilt-free by the sea.

cultivated plants appear to coexist happily, let them be. Only intervene when necessary.

Introducing native vegetation where possible—if none is present—is a great way to keep the coastal garden carefree (see p. 69). There are many wildflowers growing along roadsides and ditches that draw attention. Yes, they may be the "overachievers" that Jodi DeLong (*Plants for Atlantic Gardens*) refers to. I agree that certain plants are so successful inland that they tend to take over. But this is often precisely the kind of plant resilience needed to make it by the sea. To me, if a plant that has visual appeal can thrive here, it is a novelty.

Gardening is a verb. It does imply a little work, but it should feel like a pleasant pastime: a creative outlet involving a play of colours, textures, and shapes that complement the existing palette that nature has handed us. There is always some winnowing involved. A certain amount of selective pulling out is needed. This is essentially an act of creativity. We make visual decisions about where a certain plant is pleasing or not. Pick some and leave some. Make it a meditative part of the day. This passage about weeding by Merilyn Simonds in her book *A New Leaf: Growing with my Garden* rings so true:

A mixed blessing. But then, what blessing isn't mixed? There is no escaping it. If you garden, you weed. I don't mind really. If it weren't for the weeds, I might gaze at the garden only from a distance, like seeing loved ones from a passing train. Weeding forces me in closer.

Gardeners feel a great sense of satisfaction knowing that their piece of paradise is something they have created in cooperation with Mother Nature. However, some garden styles, in particular those of a formal nature, require far too much work and are too fragile for seaside conditions. What you plant and how the garden is arranged make a big difference to the amount of maintenance required (for more see chapter 5).

This old dory's final resting place is home to self-seeding plants that, to some, are considered weeds. Why buy yellow blooming flowers when buttercups give us a free display?

Let the sea steal the show.

A Swell Thought

The seaside gardener's prized wildflower may indeed be the inland gardener's invasive weed.

WORK LESS, LIVE MORE

Those who decide to settle by the sea do so with the intent to unwind. No matter the nature of the coastline, we find joy in simple seaside activities. Some lend themselves to a good foot massage by a barefoot walk in the sand. If the shore is adorned with a pebble beach, we go rockhounding for sea eggs, hearts of stone, and other rock novelties. A refreshing swim, a boat ride, or simply dipping our toes in cold, salty water are all pleasant distractions from the rigours of everyday life. We dine outside with family and friends at each opportunity. We go for strolls in the yard with wine in hand and take in the carefree ambiance of the seaside setting.

According to *Coastal Living* magazine, it's been proven that sand between the toes relieves stress. This chapter is, in some ways, about letting go of intensive gardening chores to make the most of life at the shore. I endorse a healthy blend of *laissez-faire* and tending the garden that will afford you time to play without feeling guilty. By the sea, the concept of negligence need not enter your mind. Relax and have some fun!

There is so much more to having fun at the shore than building sandcastles. Just about any pencil and paper game can be adapted to a sandy seaside setting.

Sea eggs

Time at the beach is always time well spent

Beach tic-tac-toe for example, is played by drawing the crossing vertical and horizontal lines in the sand and using clam and mussel shells instead of X's and O's. Ask the kids for other ideas. How about hangman? Group games at the beach are memory makers. They go along with family and friends, singsongs, fish tales, ghost stories, and great clam and corn boils over an open fire. These are people-nature bonding events. An e-device time out. Make it a time for just you and nature. Memorable experiences of the coastal environment foster a sense of value for the sea and as a result, an urgency to preserve it for future generations to enjoy. Positive experiences at the coast are much more powerful than being preachy about conservation.

To conclude, embrace the term *carefree*. Live in the garden and at the shore. Take time to relax by the sea with family and friends. Make memorable moments with them. Only tend to the garden in a leisurely manner. Let the sea and its resident creatures steal the show. That is what coastal gardening is all about.

12

Microclimates With a View

My garden like my life seems to me every year to want correction and require alteration.

—Alexander Pope—

"Microclimate" is a real buzzword in gardening these days. And to Maritime gardeners, especially those living by the sea, it is a very important one. There are zones within zones to be found in any landscape, but at the shore, climate differences can be all the more extreme. My place goes from plant hardiness zone 4a in some areas, to zone 7 in others (highest near the compost pile)! The temperature can rise by as much as 10 degrees Celsius (50 degrees Fahrenheit) just around the corner, where sea air is less direct. When it is 20 degrees Celsius (68 degrees Fahrenheit) at the shore, it can easily be as warm as 30 degrees Celsius (86 degrees Fahrenheit) in the vegetable garden, which is on the lee side of the property. The side of a house, behind a boulder, or under a large conifer, even the base of a deck, can provide plants protection from the elements. It is important to familiarize yourself well with the coastal surroundings of your property to determine what can be planted where.

A high, utilitarian wooden fence takes away potential enjoyment of the lovely water views on the other side.

Several factors can either reduce or invite the severity of weather conditions by the sea: the direction of the sun, proximity to a foundation or a structure, wide open areas, slope of the land, predominant winds, etc. The greater the degree of protection, the greater diversity of plants that can be grown. But we should not have to put up wall-like wind barriers in order to have a garden by the sea. This wooden wall hides a stunning view of an east-facing fishing cove. While such structures have their place—for privacy and as a wind guard—it is a shame to lose a view of the water for the sake of a few plants. When it comes to seaside gardening, an ideal "microclimate" would be an outdoor space where you are able to stroll and sit among your shrubs and flowering plants without barricading yourself.

Sure, you will have to choose your days for hanging out by the sea. When the weather is favourable, you will want to go out and enjoy uninterrupted views of the water among the gardens. This can be made

Sea stone berm and native vegetation offer protection

possible by creating little sheltered spaces where your plants can grow, protected from the elements. At the shore you can find many natural defences that shield less hardy plants against the elements: on the other side of a stretch of tall grasses, inside a hedge of brambles, a cluster of native spruce trees, and boulders. Plants of a different kind grow here. Leaving a buffer of native vegetation between the sea and the gardens is an excellent first line of defence, where space allows.

Many oceanfront properties, however, are too small to consider letting nature take over, but we can mimic other, more space-efficient microclimates that plants take advantage of at the shore. If you have ever come across a piece of driftwood, an old lobster trap, or a section of what once was a boat that has been there for a while, look at what is growing. The plants there may not be growing anywhere else: they have landed into a safe haven, a mini-microclimate.

A lobster trap gives these pinks a break from scorching onshore winds

This should inspire some ideas for mimicking what happens naturally at the coast.

LITTLE SEASIDE SHELTERS

It doesn't take much of a shelter to create a spot with its own unique zone characteristics. Some coastal gardeners have come up with brilliant ways to create little "outdoor rooms." These strategies include taking advantage of natural, found materials, such as stone and driftwood, that blend beautifully with the surrounding marine scenery. The following are not necessarily novel ideas, but worth sharing for their simple, enchanting beauty.

Among rocks and boulders

Local stone gives the seaside garden an air of rugged resilience. It acts as a solid wind buffer that allows a greater diversity of plants to take hold in the fiercest of seascapes. A large boulder can also anchor roots and prevent the kind of permanent lean seen so often along shorelines.

Against and around driftwood

Using driftwood is an easy and inexpensive way to create little shelters for less hardy plants, like this clump of pink penstemon (right), a delicate perennial that is prone to dropping its flowers easily. Protection from onshore winds also helps extend the blooming time of perennials, but annuals especially

A piece of driftwood shelters a delicate perennial plant called pink penstemon

Although a bit unkempt, a stone berm protects this marvellous little sitting area from fierce southwest winds.

Spring Siberian squill emerges through a fanciful wooden beach-find

benefit from a little woody shelter. Bleached wood from the shore always brings nautical charm to the coastal garden.

Structures

The corner of a house, against a shed, or inside a privacy fence: these are all ideal spots to grow tall favourites at the coast that would otherwise get flattened or shredded by strong ocean winds. A perfect spot for foxgloves is in the shelter of this wooden shed (right), where they are not only protected but they also get just the right amount filtered light.

Climbing vines cannot tolerate direct hits from the sea. A grapevine enjoys the airy protection of an attached pergola, where its large, juicy, purple grapes

Foxgloves enjoy the protection of a garden shed

Sun-loving grapes growing over a pergola ripen as they hang in safety from wind, salt spray, and predators.

hang down, sheltered from birds and wind. This is easy grape picking.

However, when planting vines, shrubs, or trees near a structure, be sure to keep a plant's mature size in mind. Wind can cause the branches of even young plants to whip the sides of a structure, which, in the case of a house, will result in wear and tear to siding and sleepless nights from unnerving noise. And once established, some vines, shrubs, and trees can be difficult to move and you run the risk of fatally injuring them in the process.

AT THE BASE OF STEPS AND DECKS

Plants soften the hard edges of steps and decks. At the same time, these utilitarian structures provide them

This elaborate deck with built-in planters keeps soil warm and plants thriving by the sea.

Perennial Johnson's Blue geraniums enjoy a safe opening where deck meets house.

with cover to get an early start despite inhospitable coastal winds. Deer love hostas, but won't use steps to access them. Where a deck comes directly against the house, leave an opening with good soil and plant a beauty that would otherwise struggle without protection. This perennial geranium, called Johnson's Blue (left), always looked ragged on the other side of the deck. Once I moved it here, to an opening in the deck, it flourished like never before!

Alongside an old dory or retired lobster traps

A structure as large as a dory has a different microclimate on each side. Our property came with an old storm-damaged cape islander hauled up and abandoned on the shore (see p.90) We moved it to the centre of the circular driveway for a nautical-themed

Even a broken wooden lobster trap can give garden plants a break.

centrepiece, but also to house some of our favourite plants. I planted several perennials around it that have different blooming times. This way, there is always a plant at its peak of colour in our driveway "island." Since the old derelict boat is so visually interesting, we don't notice when the perennials have finished their show, or the coexisting native vegetation. This garden takes care of itself (see Japanese iris show, p. 224).

An old lobster trap, although much smaller than a reclaimed boat, still provides a little casual haven for wildflowers. Even when broken up from a hard landing on the shore, old lobster traps like this one (above) provide quaint shelters for flowering garden plants.

In the shelter of larger plants

Native trees and shrubs, if you are fortunate to have them, are a great maintenance-free guard against harsh winds and salt spray. If your waterfront property is barren, consider using foundation plants to create a

These trees provide a much-needed wind barrier for majestic wisteria (p. 221).

"green fence." Evergreen trees and hedge shrubs are best suited to serve this purpose as they take well to pruning. Keeping the green fence waist-high will allow you to enjoy views of the water while providing shelter for your precious garden plants and foundation plants, but they should be started young at the coast (see chapter 3). They will need two to three years to fill out enough to become a good buffer for less hardy garden flowering plants. This process takes some forethought, though. We have to resist the urge to plant flowers before the hedge to get some colour right away. A greater diversity of plants will be able to thrive in a protected spot that would have otherwise been far too hard on them.

FIVE GARDEN-FRIENDLY SEASIDE HOMES

There was no need for me to venture far from home to find material for this section. I have the great fortune of living in a seaside community where people value gardens. The simplicity of these coastal residences is uplifting. For all the challenges of gardening by the sea, I have met with few who say that nothing can be grown here. Instead, I have discovered here a spirit of determination like no other. These folks are deeply committed to their coastal gardens and truly enjoy gardening as a rewarding, heart-healthy pastime.

It is here that I feature inspiring seaside gardens and the brilliant gardeners who created them. Each of these properties has a character and flavour of its own. Those properties that were established a generation or more ago are quite magical, and all capture a certain coastal spirit that is unique to Maritime life. These are awe-inspiring spaces where both garden and gardener grow together alongside the majestic Atlantic Ocean.

KIP HARRIS, PADDY'S HEAD

Architect Kip Harris and his wife, Marina, live in an attractive historic home that they have restored,

Kip's trees and tall shrubs, in the path of ocean winds and salt spray, give way to lavender as luscious as that grown in inland France.

Islands of colour hugged by stone and trees

expanded, and freshened up. Terraced gardens gently lead to captivating views of Indian Harbour in Paddy's Head, Nova Scotia. As with many older homes with good bones, the grounds came with impressive stonework: solid granite and flagstone retaining walls, slate steps, borders, and walkways. Each path guides us to various parts of the property. Every garden bed has a focal point: a mature tree here, a massive boulder there, a heritage flowering shrub at one end, and, of course, views of the water. The property is perched up high enough to see the open Atlantic Ocean to the left and sparkling St. Margarets Bay, with its rolling hills and ledges of white granite plunging to the sea, on the right. This magnificent setting was a good foundation from which Kip gained inspiration to get gardening by the sea and add his own touches.

Uncommon ground covers and shrubbery appear among old standards. These perennial beds, islands of colour, are impeccably cared for. Here, I move easily with my camera, not knowing quite what to expect at each turn. An arbor entices guests onto an intriguing footpath toward a little coastal meadow of grasses, wildflowers, tall bushes, and alders.

Free, rambling fireweed is adopted as part of the general garden family

Native plants and flowers take centre stage on this part of the property. Tall alders, viburnum, laurel, and wild purple asters mingling among native grasses create a casual coastal aesthetic and slow down brisk ocean-borne winds. We forget about everything else for a moment. The solitude has us take time to marvel and appreciate the diversity of plants growing so near to the sea. We re-enter the garden along a boggy section of the property. Even here there is something to please the eye. Clusters of mauve Siberian irises cohabit harmoniously with native blue flag irises. This is a garden marvel with year-round interest. Even during the dull, cold months of winter, this property has curb-by-the-sea appeal.

Shirley's laburnum tree in bloom during a foggy spell

SHIRLEY PARKS, PADDY'S HEAD

This is a postcard-perfect seaside garden. The plants growing around this small historic house elevate it to the status of a coastal cottage resort. The property has salt water on three sides and an enviable view of Paddy's Head lighthouse. When I first met

With a bit of winter protection, Shirley manages to grow spectacular blue-as-can-be hydrangeas at the coast.

Daylilies sway in the sea breeze

Shirley Parks, she was a live-in caretaker for her elderly mother, Mary Covey. A work in progress over many decades, it is surprising what Shirley is able to grow here. Never have I seen hydrangea blossoms so healthy and so intensely blue at the coast. Who would have believed that a laburnum, with its fragile links of yellow flowers, could thrive this close to the sea? This garden seems to break all the rules. Unexpected specimens thrive here. But I must mention that Shirley's plants are given the utmost care and protection to make it through our harsh coastal winters.

There is always something in bloom in this garden. When I asked Shirley how her family accumulated so many beautiful perennials, her answer was sweet and simple. One Father's Day, she wondered what to get her dad that he would really appreciate. There was no point to buying him something for his boat—the ol' fisherman had all he needed in that respect. But he did like to see plants in the yard; it was a nice change from life at sea. Shirley then made it a tradition to continue buying him a prize perennial plant each year on Father's Day. This garden is, in some ways, a tribute to her late father, Walter Covey. It is an accumulation of thoughtfully chosen shrubs and perennials over the period of his life in that little house. Today, Shirley enjoys delightful established gardens overlooking the waters of St. Margarets Bay, and so do those of us who walk by.

Azalea, juniper, and various types of spruce thrive in sea air

Exotic spruce focal point

WALTER OSTRUM /GABRIELLE APPLEBAULM AND RAFI LICHT, INDIAN HARBOUR

What began as a holiday rental turned into a dream come true. Gabrielle Applebaum and Rafi Licht, of Philadelphia, were smitten when they first laid eyes on this place, and eventually became the new owners of this Nova Scotian seaside masterpiece. The creator of this spectacular park-like Indian Harbour setting is ceramics artist Walter Ostrum. Forty years ago, this was nothing more than a windswept, barren field at the mouth of the Atlantic. But little by little, the

This filtered-light shed for propagating rhododendrons is as decorative as it is utilitarian.

ordinary one-hectare (two-acre) seaside lot was transformed by an artful introduction of exquisite trees and shrubs (see before and after pictures pp. 96–97).

These lush, established gardens have attracted much attention. Of particular interest is the collection of azalea and rhododendrons that Walter propagated in his filtered-light sheds. Those fortunate enough to get a tour will be surprised at every turn. The now established garden of mostly trees and shrubs is a labyrinth of pathways to the shore. Although the sea can only be seen from the upper decks of the house, one is always aware of its presence. While meandering through the amazing collection of familiar and unusual plants, sounds of crashing waves and seagulls and a salty fragrance fill the air. A thick hedge of tall native flora between sea and garden has been allowed to grow over the years. It now serves as a barrier from scorching winds and salt spray: an ideal coastal microclimate, able to support a variety of exotic plant specimens. A little pebble path leads to an opening on the shore where one is rewarded with sweeping views of the bold Atlantic. This oceanside garden is truly a rare and memorable experience that touches all the senses.

There is no such thing as a dull day in Olga's seaside garden.

OLGA AND VERN FREDRICKS, WINDSWEPT, MIDDLE POINT COVE

This adorable old homestead has remained in the Fredricks family for over two hundred years. Olga and Vern Fredricks have been careful to retain its original Nova Scotia coastal charms. The views of the open Atlantic on one side and the protection of Middle Point Cove on the other make for a breathtaking, authentic Nova Scotian home-by-the-sea experience. Olga is a visual artist who derives her inspiration from the coastal lifestyle that surrounds the property, and she is as creative in the garden as she is on canvas. Every plant has been thoughtfully and artfully placed

Even crevices in granite bedrock become a plant-friendly environment by the sea.

The hand of a visual artist is present at every turn.

around boulders and bare slabs of granite bedrock. Here and there, native plants and wildflowers are allowed a little spot among choice garden plants. Clusters of blooming balsam, wild purple asters, native beach roses, and tall beach grasses abound. Olga's casual gardening style gives the property a quintessential seaside flare.

A coastal chorus permeates this place. Sounds of sea breezes, fishing vessels, and social gulls add Maritime drama to this garden by the sea. Every exposed side of the lot is cloaked in hardy cascading junipers. It is a testament to how plants with coastal characteristics (see p. 23) are as graceful as they are rugged.

Susan's favourite perennials

DR. ROGER AND SUSAN MORIN, INDIAN HARBOUR

I am drawn up this red rose-lined driveway not only by the garden plants, but by the approaching views of sea, sky, and stone—spectacular! An ornamental lighthouse at the centre of the circular driveway celebrates life by the sea and hosts a few salt- and wind-tolerant plants: sea thrift, creeping Jenny, bugleweed, pinks, a beach rose bush, a false cypress, and tall ornamental grasses.

Located just around the bend from scenic Peggys Cove, Nova Scotia, Dr. Roger Morin's newly constructed seaside home was designed to complement the surrounding coastal scenery. Nearby fish stores, wharves, and the rugged coastline are what drew he and his wife Susan, the gardener in the family, to this area. To keep a garden in such an exposed location poses many challenges, but this was not a deterrent to Susan's gardening ambitions.

Little lighthouse centrepiece in an island garden

The old ice house foundation and pergola

There are several microclimates to take advantage of here. Susan makes use of spaces between and around carefully placed natural granite stone to grow a variety of tough by-the-sea perennials: astilbe, beebalm, azalea, climbing hydrangea, witches' broom, honeysuckle, and tall sedum, to name a few. The discovery of an old ice house foundation on the lot was a bonus. Here was a perfect plant- and people-friendly microclimate. This has turned into a tranquil spot to enjoy life outside, sheltered from episodes of fierce, cold Atlantic winds. A pergola perched above the stone foundation filters intense coastal sunlight. Hanging flowerpots spill their blooms and foliage around the structure like garlands, adding a touch of coziness to the outdoor, sunken stone room. Nothing softens hard edges better than plants. Another pleasant surprise was the 3 m- (10 ft.) high granite ledge that backs the property. Free of north-borne winds, this microclimate provides Susan with an easy-to-manage spot for growing a few herbs and wildflowers by the sea.

13

NAUTICAL GARDEN ACCENTS

We are as near to heaven by sea as by land.
—Humphrey Gilbert—

As if the view weren't enough, some of us like to give the seaside garden a little coastal flare, a little something nautical to add character and year-round interest. How better to celebrate life by the ocean than with memorabilia of the sea in the coastal garden? Nautical accents will set one garden apart from the rest. We can get away with a lot here at the coast without the risk of being "tacky." As long as it is reminiscent of the sea or made of natural coastal materials, it is perfectly acceptable. Keeping it "local" is key. I emphasize this because not all treasures are suited to coastal ambiance, especially those finds from travels abroad. Dutch windmills, elephant and lion ornaments, or Disney cartoon characters, for instance, are best appreciated in a special room in the house rather than in the seaside garden (I am surely stepping on a few salty toes here).

Whimsical, handcrafted folk art is fitting for coastal gardens.

Beach finds can inspire little crafty compositions

Another angle certain seaside gardeners take is to incorporate locally made folk art into the garden. The Maritimes boast a wealth of artisans whose craft "fits" the coastal setting. Given that there is so much wind at the coast, wonky wind chimes and whirligigs are popular and some are quite humorous. We here at the coast know how to have fun. Pieces that may border on the ridiculous somehow work better here than they would on the deck of a city condo, for example. Such folky pieces work well in the seaside setting, I think, because the ocean is itself whimsical in what it drops off.

The purpose of this chapter is to show what the coastal gardeners I admire have done. Many are artists. This section is meant to inspire, to offer ideas and possibilities for capturing the lure of the sea in the coastal garden. Simple objects can express a romance with the sea and the wonderful lifestyle that goes with it. We find at the shore all kinds of relics of human activity. You can't go wrong with reclaimed fishing gear: retired old wooden lobster traps, buoys, cork or glass fish floats, nets, an old lifesaver ring. Arrange these items in a spot of the garden or deck to look as if they landed themselves there or create little lighthearted compositions among potted plants. Have fun, and don't be afraid to move your seashore finds around. They can be used to distract from depleted perennials or to brighten up winter garden doldrums.

Beach stones are fascinating, and vary in colour, form, and texture from shore to shore. Seaside gardeners marvel at the smoothest ones, which add interest to a corner of the garden, little nautical touches to ordinary situations, and inspire crafty ideas.

And then there are those beach finds that sculpting waves have formed into intriguing shapes that speak to us on an emotional level. Such novel items, carved by sea and time, deserve a special spot where they won't go unnoticed: leaning against a potted plant on the deck, on an outdoor windowsill above your perennials, in a window box, on the picnic table.

Reclaimed fishing gear is in keeping with the seaside setting.

I have a collection of "hearts of stone" that get moved around often.

The Atlantic is an eccentric artist, an incidental sculptor of stone and of wood. We are eager to give our beach finds a place in the coastal home and garden. The best time to go beachcombing is immediately following a storm. Try to get out first at the crack of dawn if you find yourself on a well-frequented beach. On an average day, the best time to go is after a high tide, when little treasures get flipped above the high-water mark, especially when the wind has been strong. Found objects at the shore are a reminder that the sea is full of secrets. You will feel so privileged to have been revealed one or two.

A simple sea stone in the shape of an artist's palette.

COASTAL CULTURE IDEAS WITH YEAR-ROUND INTEREST

Another reason for having nautical objects of interest in the garden is that they can draw attention away from the "down periods" of the seaside garden. Plants have their time in the spotlight for a while, and then must undergo a period of rest. Many glorious early spring and summer perennials must lay down their wares for next year's show. When they do, some starting their spent phase as early as June, they leave a tired-looking patch of ground. And then there is that

Despite its weight, a heart-shaped granite stone is an irresistible find, well worth carrying up to the seaside garden.

drab dieback look of winter. Expressive remnants of trees, their bleached limbs and roots, give year-round interest to the coastal garden.

Driftwood can be much more than just tree parts—wood floats: handmade items made of wood wash up on beaches all the time. These are truly valuable! Ask any antique dealer. They will tell you that old wooden crates, fish-gutting tables, tool boxes, and wood paddles all bring in a good price. My prized treasure is a lid from an old chest, which showed up on my shore a few days after the infamous Hurricane Juan in September 2003 (p. 211)

The age-old tradition of using hand-painted wooden buoys to mark lobster traps and nets at sea is a dying craft. Used wooden buoys have increasingly become considered antiques since Styrofoam floats came on the scene. Lost at sea after serving an important service in someone's livelihood, an authentic, well-worn buoy tells a story. Each fishing vessel has its buoys painted a certain way for identification, a signature of sorts. Some have more than one colour. Some have initials carved into them. The colour of one of our local fishers is red: red house, red truck, red fish store, and of course, red buoys.

Landed wooden lobster traps, especially the dome-shaped traps, are another find that is becoming increasingly rare. What is most often found landed on beaches these days are the square, wire mesh traps coated in plastic to reduce corrosion. So a beached, handcrafted wooden trap is a precious find indeed.

What to do with those inflated rubber floats, also known as "markers," that show up on our shores? Never, ever discard them! Their vibrant colours work

Coastal Tip

Whenever you come across an amazing shell that is no longer living but still smelly from decomposition, place it over an ant nest. In little more than a week it will be squeaky clean, free of odours, and ready to put on display—even in the house!

Moon shell

A whale of a welcome for guests and a buoy birdhouse for feathered friends

A cluster of floats brighten up a seaside setting where nothing can grow

This old chest top is a novel idea for a deck by the sea.

COASTAL TIP

Beachcombers should keep in mind that it is a violation under the *Beaches Act* to remove any natural materials found on beaches. Shells, starfish, and sand dollars are living creatures. Never remove them live. When found below the high-water mark, they are likely still alive. You are permitted to pick them up and put them in the water where they belong. As for an interesting piece of driftwood, a shell, a rock or two, well..."Don't ask, don't tell." There is room for nature enthusiasts to collect respectfully and responsibly.

There certainly comes debris we would rather not see at the shore, notably plastics. Do pick these up immediately and discard safely. For the most part, though, the tides drop off items that both charm and mystify.

Sand dollars

well in places where plants have died back or cannot grow in storm surge-prone areas. Be sure to secure them though, or they will be lost when the next storm hits.

SEASIDE WALKWAYS, BOARDWALKS, AND PATHS

What invites curiosity more than an inspiring promenade that curves like a meandering stream with a destination? There is nothing new about walkways, boardwalks, and paths, but a trail by the sea somehow deserves special mention. Seaside walkways entice us ahead and call us to "seas" the moment; they grant us permission to come ashore and are a gracious way of showing us where to step and what to explore without fear of trampling over precious plants.

Whether a path to the shore or to the seaside garden, a walkway design can be as simple as a narrow footpath through coastal vegetation or as elaborate as flagstone set in concrete. Both designs require some planning around views of the water, sensitive areas, interesting focal points, and garden beds. Walkways, for example, add more interest to a coastal property than a flat lawn ending at a linear man-made seawall. They provide easy access to the shore in its natural state, and bring us close to particular plants that we might otherwise miss. Artist Georgia O'Keeffe wrote: "When you take a flower in your hand and really look at it, it's your world for a moment." This is a quote that really speaks to me. It sums up what gardening is all about. I am always baffled by the immense colour combinations and possibilities of flowers, and to think that something so marvellous can grow so close to the wild, moody ocean makes a little flower seem all the more miraculous.

Walkways should lead to places of interest. A little place to sit for a while encourages contemplation through all of the senses: the softness of lamb's ear, the aroma of thyme in the moist sea air, and the sound of sea breezes whispering though roses. Here you will take time to stroll slowly and marvel at sparkling diamonds of water droplets on the scalloped chartreuse leaves of lady's mantel. The sound of lapping waves and playful gulls will not be taken for granted. A path

A path of woolly thyme leads to a sitting area

that takes you to a bluff of juicy wild blackberries or blueberries growing by the shore will complete the feast of the seaside experience. I have had the great fortune of walking through several seaside gardens. These are a few of my most memorable passages with true coastal ambiance along the magnetic Atlantic Ocean. They have been divided into five categories: simple seaside footpaths, boardwalks, solid/stone walkways, natural seaside steps, and finally, seaside borders and walls.

Simple Seaside Footpaths

A footpath, in the sense of a "beaten path" is a walkway carved directly into the landscape. It is the simplest and most economical way of getting around an oceanfront property. It carefully and respectfully navigates us through sensitive areas of coastal vegetation. Footpaths are important for guiding visitors along rather than letting them venture all over the place, putting unique coastal plants and potential bird-nesting areas at risk. Footpaths are typically openings through natural coastal settings. Nothing is removed or planted; obstacles are just pushed aside just enough for us to get through with minimal interference to natural vegetation. Footpaths at water's edge tend to be temporary as storms can cause nearby stones and other natural coastal materials to shift. Every spring, touch-ups are needed. Footpaths in low-lying areas that are prone to storm surges, too, are temporary. It is best not to invest much into them. Make the best of what is there since the next storm can potentially take it out.

In areas safe from flooding and storm surges, it is well worth putting more time, money, and effort

A casual path to the sea through native coastal vegetation is refreshing.

An easy footpath through beach grass

Storm surge-prone areas are kept simple. They are temporary.

into a permanent walkway. A path of natural coastal materials with extra-strength landscaping fabric at its base makes for a most charming and inviting coastal walkway.

Any natural corridor to the beach is a stroll of a different kind, a place of repose and contemplation. It diverts our attention away from certain occasional troubles. The saying "a doctor cures, nature heals" is

It's well worth putting more effort into a path that is safe from the threat of storm surges.

well tested here at the coast. There is a lovely cottage across the cove from where we live. Part of its charm is that it is surrounded by waist-high natural coastal vegetation, with occasional clusters of mid-sized spruce trees. Were the property entirely lawn, it wouldn't have the same spirit of the sea—and we would have to listen to a lawn mower a little too often. Such modest paths to the sea are refreshing and admirably coastal in style. A narrow grassy aisle that bends gently toward the shore will add "curve appeal" to your seaside setting. Creating it involves nothing more than a maintained elbow-to-elbow opening with the help of a Whippersnipper once or twice each season. There are plenty of "urban yards" with flat, square, monoculture lawns. Dare to be different at the coast.

Boardwalks

The classic connector from land to shore is certainly the boardwalk. It is the hallmark of coastal living. A boardwalk typically follows the shoreline, taking us safely over the uneven, rocky terrain so typical of Maritime coastlines. Installing a boardwalk above the ordinary high-water mark does not require a permit, and seaside planks need no special treatment.

Salt spray acts as a natural wood preservative

Wraparound deck boardwalk makes room for honeysuckle

Coastal Tip

A permit is required from the Department of Fisheries and Oceans to make any alterations below the regular high-water mark. Oceanfront homeowners can apply for a 4.5 m- (15 ft.) wide skid, a traditional wooden slide from which a boat can be dragged in and out of the water, but this space need not necessarily be a "skid." You may clear enough rock in that space to have a small people-friendly beach.

Salt spray acts as a wood preservative and a natural insecticide against ant infestations, but it is important to have good-sized gaps between the planks to maintain airflow. The gaps also allow debris to fall through rather than clog up and retain moisture that eventually leads to rot. If done well, planks can last for decades. The thicker the cut of wood, the longer it will last.

Five-cm- (2-in.) thick rough-sawn pine planks are relatively inexpensive and actually more durable than thinner, chemically treated pine, which leaches into the environment. Cedar planks, rich in natural oils, are about the same price as treated wood and age to a beautiful, long-lasting silvery-grey at the coast. This wood is insect resistant and poses no harm to the environment, unlike the slow-release chemical concoction of treated wood.

Never use treated wood around food crops or where people will walk barefoot. A good alternative is to dip untreated pine or spruce boards in an organic, boron-based product called LifeTime, available in any hardware store. It comes in a powder form that is easily diluted in water. Because boron is a naturally occurring compound, there is no worry about walking barefoot on wood treated with it, or of contaminating the environment. It gives wood products outdoor longevity, deters insects, and best of all, gives wood the even, silvery-grey sheen of driftwood in just a few months.

Solid / Stone Walkways

Depending on how much one is willing to spend, stone or concrete surfaces are the most permanent and maintenance-free seaside walkways. There are many concrete composites to pick from these days. Some are interlocking geometrical shapes and others are less structured. Flagstone is the most popular natural stone option. There are several methods for laying it down, with different results.

Flagstone set in concrete requires prepping the ground with a thick layer of at least 10 cm (4 in.) of crushed gravel to prevent frost heave. This is a job best done by a skilled landscaping company as the stone slabs come in slight variations of thickness. The slabs must also be cut with a special saw to fit into one another in order to achieve defined edges. While it is beautiful and lasts a lifetime, it is also pricey. Flagstone can also be set, in the same way, directly over crushed gravel and only the cracks filled in with a

Flagstone set in concrete is durable and maintenance free, but pricey.

gritty concrete mix to prevent vegetation from growing through. Over time, cracks do occur and the fill mix breaks down, but it is easily replenished.

Thankfully, there are low-budget alternatives when using flagstone. To begin, if you can access leftover stone from a job site, this is a great savings. Alternately, some gardeners set flagstones over pea gravel and landscape fabric. However, landscaping cloth is not resistant enough to keep aggressive vegetation from coming through, so some weeding will be needed. Leftover roofing shingles keep weeds out well: just fill in the cracks between stones with sand or crushed gravel, but be ready to tolerate a bit of winter heave.

Gardeners with a good eye can lay down pieces loosely to make attractive stepping stones to various parts of the seaside garden, adding topsoil in between them. If well-travelled, only low-growing vegetation can establish itself between the stones. If you have a mossy spot, flat stones are ideal because the moss makes a lovely natural fill. Finally, do not limit the possibilities to natural stone. Brick, especially old salvaged bricks, make a great "country cottage style" walkway. Commercial patio stones, too, in all their many shapes, can keep coastal walkways open.

Flat-sided stones from the site were placed as steps to the shore during excavation.

NATURAL SEASIDE STEPS

It is always wise to build a coastal home high above sea level, but this can require extensive stairs to the shore and garden. There are many options to getting down and around to the seaside gardens and to the water. The most durable and maintenance-free steps with a coastal flare are those of natural stone. Flat stepping stones could meander down the slope if it isn't too steep—keeping in mind that now and then, you'll have to use a weed whacker to keep the steps passable.

Some coastal properties come with stony "gifts." Where just a few stones are needed, look to the shore. Natural flat stones are not uncommon and are often quite portable. Choose stones wide enough to accommodate a large man's foot: large stones make a great coastal focal point as well as great steps. Stony gifts may be just below the surface. During excavation for a new house, have all large boulders set aside, especially flat-sided stones. Have them integrated into the landscape or installed for steps while the machinery is on site. If none are found on site, large quarried stones can be purchased for commercial and residential use.

Stone blocks retain a gritty walking surface and create natural landings.

A flat, local granite stone serves as a sturdy step up to the house entrance.

Flat stones make a tidy, easy-to-maintain edging.

SEASIDE BORDERS AND WALLS

Borders, edging, and retaining walls are utilitarian. There is a temptation to use commercial materials for an easy fix, but these are not necessarily in keeping with the seaside setting. One homeowner needed a way to keep gravel from being spilled into the garden during snow removal. A long driftwood pole found on the shore offered an ideal solution. It was cut into several pieces and used to line the little seaside garden (see p. 220).

Found objects of wood and stone can serve an important purpose while also echoing the charms of the sea. An effect of coastal drama can be achieved by creating contrast: high against low, flat against

A path of old reclaimed bricks contrasts well against seaside greenery.

hilly, soft against hard, liquid against solid, and so on. When border and path are juxtaposed in opposite ways, we forget about function. We are rather taken by the visual impact of the materials.

Whimsical seaside accents along the way can also become part of the border. An old fish crate filled with rope, buoys, or a bunch of bleached driftwood sticks is an easy way to retain the spirit of the sea. Incorporate lighting for evening strolls. Free-standing solar-powered lights are very popular and come in many styles, from traditional to fun.

A driftwood post border prevents gravel from being pushed into the garden during snow removal.

Solar-powered lights mounted on wharf posts with rope suit the seaside setting well.

A retaining wall of local stone adds drama to the seaside garden

Cornerstone's old-growth wisteria

CORNERSTONE BY THE SEA: BILL GIMBY

The aptly named "Cornerstone" homestead is a truly unique coastal property found just outside of Hubbards, Nova Scotia. Artisan, builder, and renovator Bill Gimby and his wife, Bonnie, were enamoured when they first came upon this turn-of-the-century seaside cottage, about thirty years ago. The original foundation dates back to 1912. Oxen would have hauled these big old stones.

Bill got inspired to continue the tradition of building with stone. He took a course in masonry and bought himself a little cement mixer. The rest is history. One may say that Bill gardens more with stone than with plants. The property boasts impressive rock walls, borders, steps, and artistry that instill an atmosphere of permanence and endurance in the presence of the bold Atlantic Ocean.

And there are certainly gardens here. Mats of ground cover and low-growing perennials contrast brilliantly against the massive stone structures that

Coastal Tip

Natural stone is indispensable in the coastal landscape. If a lot of it is needed, visit a construction site. There is always unwanted rock during excavation that will either be buried or hauled away. You may even get it delivered for free, saving the property owner a disposal fee.

The view from Cornerstone

have been so exquisitely placed throughout the seaside setting.

Bill is also an avid beachcomber. The little crafty touches of sticks and stones quivering in the sea breeze speak of his passion for the ocean. He can make something out of anything he finds at the shore. Bill, the so-called "rock man" has a good eye, but he doesn't see himself as an artist. He says that he just does what feels "right" with his beach finds. All of his pieces are infused with the lure of the sea. They are so fitting for seaside gardens, and are especially appreciated during the winter months.

Bill's beach finds, waiting to become artifacts for enthusiasts

Bill Gimby has a natural flare for turning simple beach finds into sea-inspired coastal crafts.

Bill's Gimby's nautical work is an homage to the sea and to maritime living. He has difficulty keeping up with demand for his coastal indoor and outdoor crafts, which are sold throughout Nova Scotia and the US Eastern seaboard. Above are just a few of his signature pieces.

Bill's amazing, free-spirited arrangements of beach finds

Appendix

Tried-and-True Coastal Garden Plants

Japanese irises

We began our journey into *Atlantic Coastal Gardening* on the untamed shores of Nova Scotia. Coastal vegetation can give us valuable insights into what contributes to plant resilience. Each plant in my chart of favourites has at least two or more "coastal characteristics" (p. 23). I hope gardeners will use this book to learn about *how* to choose plants for a seaside garden and how to grow them well, but in the following chart I suggest *what* to grow. This list is geared towards those for whom gardening at the coast is uncharted territory, or for those who are hesitant to try something new. Don't limit yourself to my choices. There certainly are many more suitable plant candidates for gardens by the sea that I have not yet tried.

Since bringing colour to the landscape is a big part of gardening, this chart focuses mainly on flowering plants. A few of my chosen favourites may raise eyebrows. They may seem too delicate for extreme seaside situations. Annual poppies, for instance, have shown up on their own, right down to the water's edge of our shore, likely from windblown seeds. In fact, poppies have two "coastal characteristics": silvery leaves, and stems that are also semi-succulent. The harsh climate keeps seaside poppies short and stout compared to those grown in a garden. Another example of a delicate beauty that thrives at the shore is morning glory.

Garden morning glory (left) is a relative of the lovely native bindweed (right).

Its intense, electric-blue colour is a visual magnet. I decided to try growing it because it resembles native coastal bindweed so closely. Even their seeds are indistinguishable. I recently learned that they are, in fact, related. If a garden plant that you love looks and behaves as a native coastal plant, I say go for it!

Throughout the book, I've referred to plants by their commonly accepted names rather than using botanical terms. I've done this for a couple of reasons. First, we common folk do not speak Latin. While it is the textbook language of botanists and horticulturalists, this book was written for *you*, after all, not them. However, for the purpose of seaside gardening, it is useful to know that Latin plant names prefixed with *maritima* or *marinus* signify plants found to do well at the shore. It is an indication of a native coastal plant or a plant that originated as one. The same applies to common plant names with the prefix "sea," as in sea holly, sea thrift, sea oats, and sea lavender, for example. Finally, though plant names may differ regionally, these days, you need only go online to find other given names and photos for plant identification, including scientific names, if you're interested. I would say to those few who may feel disadvantaged by the lack of scientific terminology in the book, it is not necessary to know a plant's botanical Latin name to grow it well and to enjoy it.

Seaside gardeners should find the following chart useful for planning out a garden that will have something in bloom throughout the entire growing period. The plants are listed seasonally, in order of peak performance and blooming period. Average plant height is also important in deciding what to plant where, so that shorter plants are not concealed and shaded by taller ones. Sun/shade requirements are noted so that the best location is chosen for optimal health and flower colour. Finally, a brief informative comment has been included about each plant.

Well...this is where I sign off. My garden gloves are well worn and the sea is pleasantly calm. Happy *Atlantic Coastal Gardening* to all!

Sea holly is an endearing, self-seeding perennial, well suited for rugged shorelines.

Favourite Plants	April	May	June	July	Aug.	Sept.	Oct.	Nov.	Type	Sun required	Height	Comments
Johnny jump up									A/P	☼ ⛅	12 cm (5 in.)	Self-seeds. Long-lasting, cheerful, purple-yellow faces.
pansy									A/P	☼ ⛅	15 cm (6 in.)	Behaves as perennial at coast. Comes in all colours.
lungwort									P	☼ ⛅	18 cm (7 in.)	Long-lasting flowers start pink and turn blue. Decorative foliage all season.
Siberian squill									P	☼ ⛅	12 cm (5 in.)	Small, naturalized bulbs. Intense blue, wind- and salt-tolerant blooms.
primula									B/P	☼ ⛅	10 cm (4 in.)	Comes in all colours. Can be potted. Winter protection recommended.
forget-me-not									B/P	☼ ⛅	10–15 cm (4–6 in.)	Very versatile, easily relocated. Indispensable.
creeping phlox									P	☼	3 cm (1 in.)	Great, maintenance-free ground cover. Comes in many shades of pink to red.
money plant									P	☼	30–40 cm (12–16 in.)	Striking fuchsia flowers are followed by everlasting seedpods.
seathrift									P	☼	20 cm (8 in.)	Extremely salt spray- and wind-resilient plant.
azalea									P	☼ ⛅	80 cm (2 1/2 ft.)	When in bloom, azaleas are very showy. New varieties range from orange to deep purple. Cultivars with hardiness zone 4 or less do best at the coast.
speedwell									P	☼ ⛅	15 cm (6 in.)	Brilliant blue blossom ground cover. No weeding necessary.
bugleweed									P	☼ ⛅	15 cm (6 in.)	A vigorous, carefree ground cover. Leaves come in shades of purple.
thyme									P	☼	1 cm (1/3 inch)	Several scented varieties available with varying foliage texture (i.e. woolly thyme).
cushion spurge									P	☼	30 cm (12 in.)	Long-lasting, bright yellow bracts that turn tangerine in the fall.
beach pea									A/P	☼	30 cm (11 in.)	A vigorous native that grows well from seed.
cranesbill									P	☼	25 cm (10 in.)	A great, reliable bloomer and ground cover. Transplants well.
tall phlox									P	☼	60 cm (2 ft.)	Many colour choices: white, pinks, reds, and purples. Excellent naturalization. Early and late summer varieties available.
forsythia									P	☼	1.5 m (5 ft.)	Cheerful yellow flowers smother this shrub. Plant cultivars zone 4 or lower.
snow-in-summer									P	☼ ⛅	15 cm (5 in.)	The only splash of white that cascades nicely during these months.
bachelor button									A	☼	40 cm (1 1/3 ft.)	A welcome carefree splash of true blue. Start plant inside.
weigela									P	⛅	1–2 m (3 1/3–6 1/2 ft.)	A handsome flowering shrub that can weather all that the sea throws at it.

Favourite Plants	April	May	June	July	Aug.	Sept.	Oct.	Nov.	Type	Sun Required	Height	Comments
impatiens									A		12 cm (5 in.)	A great, fog-loving plant with non-stop blooms in acidic soil.
wax begonia									A		12 cm (5 in.)	A very forgiving salt spray- and wind-tolerant little plant.
yellow loosestrife									P		30 cm (12 in.)	Cheery, tall spikes covered in cadmium yellow. They sway nicely in sea breezes.
perennial bachelor button									P		60 cm (2 ft.)	Faithful blue flowers with lovely velvet, silvery foliage.
columbine									B/P		70–80 cm (2 1/2–3/4 ft.)	Exotic-looking flowers that grow thicker each year.
chive blooms									P		40 cm (1 1/3 ft.)	This versatile herb puts on a show year after year. A garden jewel.
lupin									P		70–90 cm (2 1/3–3 ft.)	A very flexible flowering plant, even at water's edge.
bleeding-heart									P		60–70 cm (2–2 1/2 ft.)	Plant on the lee side for spectacular clusters of quivering little hearts.
clematis									P		1–2 m (3.3–6.6 ft.)	Early blooming varieties do better at the coast, and bloom again in the fall.
Johnson's Blue									P		25 cm (2.1 ft.)	A perennial, true-blue, fog-loving geranium.
yellow iris									P		60 cm (2 ft.)	Performs well even at water's edge. Divide every spring.
Japanese iris									P		80 cm (2. 6 ft.)	Tolerates acidic soil and boggy landscapes well.
daylily									P		60–80 cm (2–2 3/4 ft.)	Plant on lee side for best results. Many varieties available.
lobelia									A		10 cm (4 in.)	Great filler, tough and carefree. See p. 48 to grow from seed.
foxglove									B/P		90 cm (3 ft.)	Thrives in foggy climates and shallow, acidic soil. Colours include white, pink, blue, and purple.
creeping Jenny									P		6 cm (2 in.)	A reliable, cheerful, yellow flowering ground cover.
honeysuckle									P		Vine	Superb blooming performance even in the path of seaside drama.
beach rose									P		1.5 m (5 ft.)	These are outstanding once established. Start them young. Full sun is essential to bloom.
blue flag iris									P		1 m (3 1/3 ft.)	Hearty, showy blossoms for a time, leaving tall clusters of pods with winter interest.
dropmore									P		90 cm (3 ft.)	Tall, cobalt-blue flowers that divide easily in spring.
astilbe									P		50–60 cm (1 3/4–2 ft.)	White-pink-to-red blooms spring up like fire-works. A good all-season plant.

Favourite Plants	April	May	June	July	Aug.	Sept.	Oct.	Nov.	Type	Sun required	Height	Comments
garden yellow loosestrife									P	☀ ⛅	90 cm (3 ft.)	Lovely trumpet-shaped yellow flowers wrap around tall stems. Easy to transplant
blanket flower									P	☀	30–35 cm (1 ft.)	Extremely hardy even at water's edge. Self-seeds. Divide early spring. Very showy.
campion									B/P	☀	60 cm (2 ft.)	Long-lasting, intense fuchsia-coloured flowers on tall, sturdy stems. Also comes in white.
pink catchfly									A/B	☀ ⛅	25 cm (10 in.)	Vibrant, deep-pink blooms that weather wind and salt spray well.
monkshood									P	☀ ⛅	60 cm (2 ft.)	Carefree purple perfusion. Makes a great dramatic backdrop.
poppy									A	☀	1 m (3 1/3 ft.)	Spectacular flowers and deer deterrent. Self-seeds readily.
feverfew									A/B	☀ ⛅	20 cm (8 in.)	Hardy, sweet-smelling daisy-like flowers. Naturalizes well with native plants.
lady's mantel									P	☀ ⛅	20 cm (8 in.)	Lovely chartreuse clusters of florets that can brave the coastal elements.
creeping thyme									P	☀ ⛅	2 cm (3/4 in.)	Showy, robust ground cover. Many varieties available.
chicory									P	☀	60 cm (2 ft.)	Foliage at ground level. Bright blue, daisy-like flowers twirl on tall, stiff stems.
lavender									P	☀	20 cm (8 in.)	Fragrant flowers spike above hardy mounds of little thick, silver leaves.
beebalm									P	☀	80 cm (2 1/2 ft.)	Aromatic herb. Tolerates cool, humid soil. Many cultivars, from white to shades of pink, red, and purple.
perennial sweet pea									P	☀	1 m (3 1/3 ft.)	Similar in appearance to annual variety but only available in one shade of pink. Grows well at water's edge with native plants.
balsam									P	☀ ⛅	90 cm (3 ft.)	Great naturalized on a bank or in a meadow.
garden sedum									P	☀	4 cm (1 in.)	Drought resistant. Provide good drainage. An array of colours available.
climbing hydrangea									P	☀ ⛅	1 m (3 1/3 ft.)	Flat, white corymbs on clinging branches of dense, shiny, green leaves.
spirea									P	☀ ⛅	1.5 m (5 ft.)	Many varieties of height, flower, and foliage colour available. All zone 4 or lower.
tall sedum									P	☀	30 cm (12 in.)	Extremely wind and salt spray resistant. Available in many shades of pink.
statice									A	☀	30 cm (12 in.)	An everlasting plant. Papery blooms sparkle atop sturdy stems. All colours.
clematis									P	☀ ⛅	Vine	Late varieties bloom in September. Requires a support. Many colours available.
strawflower									A	☀	50 cm (1 3/4 ft.)	Robust, crinkly flowers in an array of bloom colours. Perfect for dried arrangements.

Favourite Plants	May	June	July	Aug.	Sept.	Oct.	Nov.	Dec.	Type	Sun Required	Height	Comments
black-eyed Susan									P	☼	30 cm (12 in.)	An undemanding old-fashioned flower that can grow anywhere.
Coreopsis moonbeam									P	☼	30 cm (12 in.)	Easy, reliable mounds of gold that sway in sea breezes. Does well in sandy soils.
nasturtium					TO FROST				A	☼	15 cm (6 in.)	A great sprawling or cascading plant that blooms profusely.
hollyhock									B	☼	50 cm (1 3/4 ft.)	An old-fashioned favourite. Best grown against a wall or trellis for support.
echinacea									P	☼	50 cm (1 3/4 ft.)	A lovely sight. These sturdy plants do well in sandy soils and windy spots.
sea holly									P	☼	50 cm (1 3/4 ft.)	Best enjoyed planted in masses. Unusual steely blue flowers and stems.
morning glory									A	☼	Vine	Brilliant sky-blue or purple varieties. Flowers close late afternoon. Requires a support.
grapevine					TO FROST				P	☼	Vine	Thrives by the sea in average soil. Puts out a profusion of grapes. Good pergola plant (see p. 193)
hops					TO FROST				P	☼ ⛅	Vine	Plants die back each year but new spring growth are vigorous and rapid. With a male plant, females produce attractive, papery, lime-green cones. A very tough vine that freely cascades or climbs.
wild purple aster									P	☼	50 cm (1 3/4 ft.)	Will grow just about anywhere. Simply cast spent flowers over preferred spots.
Montauk daisy									P	☼	1 m ()	Looks like a shrub. The last plant to bloom at the coast. Butterflies rush in for a last good helping of nectar. Large, 4 cm daisies are a pleasant surprise late in the season.
cotoneaster									P	☼ ⛅	30 cm (h) x 1 m (w) (1 ft. [h] x 3.3 ft. [w])	A robust ornamental ground cover with fall red berries that attract birds. Tolerates pruning and salt spray.
tansy					TO FROST				P	☼	1.5 m (4.11 ft.)	A tall, aromatic, naturalized plant whose button flowers work well in dry arrangements.
winterberry						TO MID-WINTER			P	☼	1–2 m (3 1/3–6 1/2 ft.)	A native plant now available as a garden-variety plant. Male and female are needed to produce red berries on female plants. A rarity: a shrub that tolerates acidic boggy soils.
Virginia creeper									P	☼ ☁	Vine	A versatile climbing vine or ground cover, appreciated for crimson fall foliage.
English ivy				ALL YEAR					P	☼ ☁	Vine	Lustrous evergreen leaves. Clings strongly to stone and concrete surfaces.
Boston ivy				ALL YEAR					P	☼ ☁	Vine	Great over boulders, concrete, and as ground cover. Superb fall foliage colour.
climbing bittersweet									P	☼ ⛅	Vine	A twining, woody vine with small green flowers that become eye-catching clusters of red fall fruit on female plants. Male plant required.
purple flowering raspberry									P	☼	1.3 m (4 1/4 ft.)	A carefree shrubby plant with dazzling long-lasting clusters of purple-red blossoms. Very wind tolerant.
red/yellow twig osier	«							»	P	☼ ⛅	2 m (6 1/2 ft.)	Bright upright stems provide much-appreciated winter colour and interest. Summer flowers are insignificant.

INDEX

Numbers in italics refer to images; bold refer to recipes.